Amusing Adventures with a Slightly Eccentric Cyclist

Cycle Touring for Lunatics

Contents

Introduction to drug smuggling

The most effective way to smuggle class A drugs into the UK is by bicycle.

24 ferries across the channel in the last few years. Not once have I been stopped, checked, or even given a suspicious, sideways glance. Just a friendly smile from the high-vis port staff. A wave on through.

Think about some of the bike-packing setups you've seen. People off on their round-the-world adventures. Looking like bringing their whole wardrobe, plus provisions to last them for months. All lashed to their bike higgledy-piggledy; bags, straps, duct tape, whatever was at hand. That's an abundance of carrying capacity for smuggling. Let's do the maths:

- Four 35 litre pannier bags.
- One 70 litre tailfin bag.
- A frame bag (fits inside the main triangle of the bicycle).
- Handlebar bags.
- Big rucksack on your back.

How much party-powder could you smuggle into the UK with all that? Thousands of pounds? Hundreds of thousands? A million? Based on the density of cocaine and its current street value......It's $30,000,000. Errrrrrrr....ok. This is a conservative estimate.

(**note to editor**: Let's bin this section. Whilst completely true, it is only written to get the attention of publishers. Publishers who are probably searching for an action-packed, explosion-filled story. Right now they're probably imagining Snatch but on bicycles*. Or Breaking Bad....Braking Bad? Anyway, book publishers aren't on the lookout for some chump on a crappy bicycle. Not even making it out of Western Europe. Where the occasional mishap occurs, but no proper peril. Those stories must be ten a penny. I'd also like this section removed for convenience. If more than several people read this, it's going to be pretty fucking inconvenient getting stopped and bag searched every single time I'm passing through Dover. As my internet search history is now filled with "*What is the density of street cocaine?*", "*How much does 1kg of cocaine cost?*", that's all the more likely).

*A note about Snatch: Not everyone has seen the film

Snatch. Important to remember that. Especially when you're getting your lunchtime wrap, the falafel-monger' asks: "*Would you like some spicy sauce on that?*"
You wittily retort: "*No thanks Turkish, I'm hot enough already*". This is potentially mildly amusing if you've seen Snatch. Potentially mildly racist if not. Straight into the top #3 of my awkward lunch encounters. Slots in right above leaning over to pay and dropping my phone into a steaming bowl of Ethiopian curry.

So I'm sorry to let you down. This is not an action-packed drug-fueled orgy of gangsters and excitement. The only drugs in this book are copious amounts of caffeine, anti-histamines, and a few magic mushrooms. If you want to keep reading, you've been well and truly warned. Hopefully you got this as a Christmas present and haven't wasted your hard earned money on it. Although if you're a road-cyclist, let's be honest, there's a good chance you already have more money than sense. I am a road cyclist, so I am allowed to say that! This is probably going to end up freely readable on Kindle anyway. More money to Mr Bezos, he needs a new superyacht I'm sure.

I've tried to make the book more than: "*I got on my bike. I cycled to <boring Belgian town>. I ate some waffles. I* *cycled some more*". But to be honest it's gotten a bit out of control. It's barely a cycling book anymore. It's just words now. So many words. Therefore if the rambling gets too overwhelming, please feel free to flick through to whichever chapters grab your attention. I won't judge you. But do not tell me that you skipped chapters to my face; I may strike you.

Enough faffing, you probably came here for some hot cycling action, so let's give you what you want and get on with the adventures.

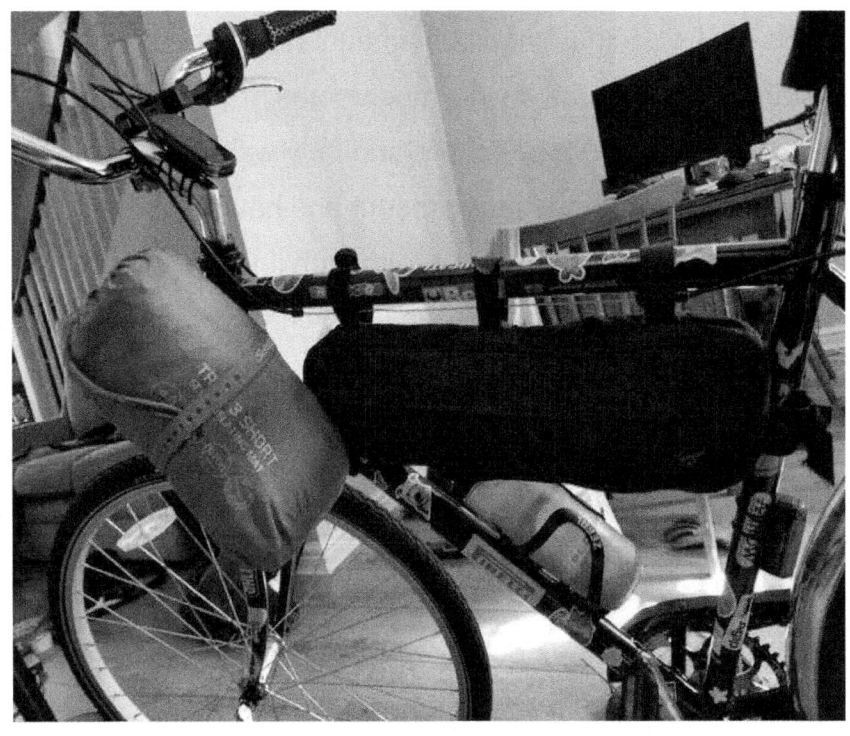

Bicycle to Berlin: The Big Plan

The Challenge:
- Take the most ridiculous and unsuitable bike you can buy…
- Pedal this silly contraption over multiple countries, and multiple hills, all the way from Canterbury to Berlin. Roughly 1000 kilometers.
- All with under 6 days to get there, because I've bought tickets to see pop-punk legend Jeff Rosenstock performing live.

The question most folks ask me about this trip was "…*Why*????", especially with regards to bike choice. I struggle to answer this…stuttering and mumbling, a different answer each time.

I don't recall ever consciously committing to the trip. It just kind of happened. One day I was thinking about Berlin, I'd seen this bike on sale, and then suddenly I'm sitting with it at the port of Dover, about to depart on this grand adventure. Guess this is happening then? ¯_(ツ)_/¯

The conscious part of your brain is capable of planning and smart decision-making. But you've always got the primitive, ancient reptilian lizard part; back there, lurking in the shadows. The lizard sits in the back, pretending it doesn't exist, but now and again you'll notice its presence. You'll get to the supermarket counter and there's a family-size bag of M&Ms in your basket. You never decided you needed or wanted M&M's, especially in such vast quantities. That was Mr Lizard. By the way, feel free to change Mr to whatever suits your Lizard.

When you're tired and drained, Mr Lizard is more active. Well it's more that the conscious part is less active. The conscious part has gone on a smoke-break, and left the Lizard at the wheel. With strict instructions to not do anything reckless. Which sometimes the Lizard-at-the-Wheel heeds. Online shopping can be pretty bad for this. Mr Lizard making questionable late night purchases. The delivery driver dropping it off a few days later. You think: *"Why the flip have I bought this again?"*. For me it's usually a new bike. I'm up to 8 now, although I genuinely do need a 9th for a winter road bike and indoor-trainer bike. I'm not joking, the cyclists reading will probably understand (**editor note**: Already 9. I need a 10th). So it was probably during one of these Lizard-at-the-Wheel evenings that I found the "joke" bike in my basket and my ferry ticket booked.

After Mr Lizard has committed you to a course of action, you may notice that your conscious brain is sheepish and embarrassed. It's a control freak, it cannot stand to admit that it isn't responsible for all of your choices. So what does the conscious part do? It works backwards, finds a way to reverse-engineer some logic. Proving to you that although it had not been in charge, it had always wanted and planned to do Mr Lizard's choice from the start. So what is happening right now is good, and there's no reason to be mad at it for going AWOL!

The post-decision, reverse-engineered logic for the Berlin adventure is a combination of many factors:
- Jeff Rosenstock was playing Berlin on his tour but not London.
- Attempting to cut down on flying: save the planet and all that jazz. I've managed to avoid flying this whole year, so where could I cycle from my house in Kent, which still feels like an adventure?
- Watching "Abroad in Japan" cycle adventures on youtube and feeling inspired/jealous.

- Getting back in contact with an old friend who lived in Berlin. Would be cool to visit.

- I yearned for a big cycling challenge. Something crazy and brutal enough I could raise some money for charity. It's difficult to raise money through activities that I actively enjoy. "*Hey, why not give me a load of money to have a nice day out on my bike*". Especially considering if I gave up those ridiculous £4 "*mini-cheescakes-in-little-glass-jars*", I could give all that cheesecake money to a good cause, without having to pester people.

- Seeing an already cheap bike heavily discounted. Love me a good deal. Slap a 75% off price sticker on anything and I will buy it. No matter how useless or inconvenient.

Mr. Lizard isn't totally random. He will often base his actions on what has been filtering into your subconscious. This is why it annoys me when people say: "*Oh, advertising has no effect on me*". Yeah, maybe not on the conscious part of your brain. But your lizard is always paying attention.

And so when all your thoughts lead to Berlin, then it feels like that's where the Universe wants you to go. And Mr Lizard makes the executive decision: We're going to Berlin!

The next thing I know...the budget bike is sitting in a massive cardboard box in my back garden next to the wheelie bins ¯_(ツ)_/¯

The Bike:

The bike. The bike was worrying. It cost £96. You could tell. Yeah it was heavily reduced, but still the cheapest new bike you can get before discounts. It's a Schwinn Wayfarer city bike. The kind of bike you'd expect to see your granny popping to the shops on with her flowery basket; not some lycrad-up, twatty-sunglasses sporting road-rider. I'd got the bike delivered to home and had to half-assemble it myself. The brakes were completely skewiff. The gears were out. The rear wheel was so buckled and wobbly it hit the frame. The drivetrain clacked. It sounded cheap. It felt cheap. It was cheap. Should I get a professional to ensure it would be safe to ride this thing nearly 500 miles? Nah! It seems piss poor economics to take a £96 bike for a £70 service. So I bodged it the best of my...how shall we say....limited.....abilities. The fact that you're reading this indicates I'm not dead (yet!).

Important things first....the stickers! It was vitally important the bike looked cool. Looked as ludicrous as the challenge it was being attempted on. First I applied a pack of motorcycle decals e.g. Rossi's "The Doctor" emblem, lots of "Castrol" and "Ducati" stickers. Against the glossy, black frame of the bike it actually looked super slick. So then I balanced it out with rainbow stickers and children butterflies. When I was finished, 90% of the frame was covered and it looked like a completely different bike.

Next: The rear wheel was so buckled and wobbly it would bump the frame as it spun round. 30 minutes of random twiddling with a spoke key eventually got it to a rideable state. Very proud of this one.

Couldn't really get the brakes to work. Quite important. Brakes that is. Procrastinated on this minor detail until two days before leaving. I finally had the genius idea of "bodging" the brake pads into the correct position by sticking a load of spare 6mm washers in the right places.

Gave up on the front mudguard. In the bin with that. Got the rear mudguard on. Only to find out it needed removing to take the rear wheel off. Turned out removing the rear wheel was a massive ball-ache due to the bolt placement. If I got a puncture it would be an absolute nightmare. A multi-hour job. So I allowed myself a single upgrade. Schwalbe

Marathon Plus tyres. If you're a cyclist these probably need no explanation. But for regular readers I'll explain: When it comes to puncture protection, these are the big daddies. Like riding with extra-safe condoms from boots. You're not gonna have a fun time with them on. But you're also not gonna have a sudden disaster on your hands. Maybe you already have children and you don't view that as a disaster. Good for you.

Note: Although I go for Marathon Plus tyres, I don't actually go for extra-safe prophylactics. I could never bring myself to "willingly" create a mini-human, but I don't think I'd be too miffed if it somehow happened by mistake. I'd probably see it as a sign from the universe, a challenge, and be willing to roll with it. If you didn't plan for it you can always say: "Well, I never asked for this. But I did my best". Lowers expectations and responsibility. A bit like when I was born. I was over a month late. I was very content where I was; zero desire to go out into the cold, cruel world. Eventually I had to be yanked out. So I never explicitly made the choice to be part of this world, therefore you're not allowed to expect anything of me; but, I'm still giving this existence thing a decent crack.

I could see myself enjoying being a parent, but the responsibility of actively wanting to have kids....what if 3 months in you realise you've made a terrible mistake? I already have huge regrets about signing up for a whole year of Duolingo. It's a very brave decision. The children one. The responsibility of being a father would also force me to begin actively avoiding prison and/or death. I don't tell people this, because it's a bit "delusions of grandeur"-y, but I would like to make the world a fairer place for everyone.....that bit's fine...but I do see myself as potentially the next Leon Trotsky. Father of the Russian revolution. That's the slightly delusional bit. And whilst he was in some ways a "*great man*"....there's no denying he was also a bit of a cunt to his family..."families"! Example: He was exiled to Siberia with his first wife; they had a couple of kids. Pretty committed right? You'd feel obligated to raise them and ensure their happiness right? Not for old Leon. He escaped; alone....which is fine... but rather than making any attempt to free them from the bitterly cold and desolate Siberia....he skedaddles to London, to go out partying with Lenin every night! As if that wasn't enough, he just casually grabs himself a brand new wife...as you do. I think my point was originally going to be about how if I've got kids, then I wouldn't be able to change the face of the world, because I wouldn't have time for both....but Trotsky might have had time for both. He was just a nob. Get an assistant. Get your assistant to break your family out of Siberian exile! Although maybe I don't actually want to change the world. Maybe I just look up to, and want to "want to be the kind of person who tries to change the world". When really all I want to do in life is ride my bikes, play my video-games and play with my willy. So it would be a convenient accident to be forced into accepting responsibility for a child. "Oh darn it. I forgot about parents evening. I guess I can't bring down the capitalist system this evening. I'll have to remember to do it when little Fenrir's away on the school skiing trip". Bit like the fingers-man from The Banshees of Inisheerin. Lifting the crushing weight of responsibility to leave a mark on the Earth, as if that mark would somehow immortalise you anyway, make your inevitable death and non-existence any less petrifying......

....I've well and truly forgotten about how any of this: the Russian revolution, the responsibilities of parenthood, or our inevitable demise....how any of it is related to bicycle tyres in the slightest? But the point is that Marathon Plus rock! I have pulled 4 inch nails out of Marathon Plus tyres. They might be heavy, but they are a beast of a tyre. Whilst riding them I laugh in the face of hedge-cuttings. I eat broken glass for breakfast. I'm unstoppable!

So despite my bike-bodging, on the paltry 2 mile test run to the shops it didn't fall apart. Good to go right?

What's on the bike?

- I've got a big tailfin pack with my tent...yes I thought it would be a good idea to camp. Yes I very much regret that. Watch out with these massive tailfin bags. When overloaded, after enough time they will eventually droop down like a pensioners breasts. They'll start skimming the wheels on every bump in an incredibly annoying manner. It's no problem on this bike because it had a built-in pannier rack, but has been a problem for me on road bike rides. You can get clamp-on pannier holder thingies. Or a mudguard can do the job, but that can just force the mudguard to rub.
- The cheapest Halfords **pannier bag** stuffed way too full with spare clothes and a sleeping bag

  - I pack **very light clothes-wise**. Only 1 extra pair of cycling gear on top of what I'll wear day 1. Cycling gear can always be "cleaned" by showering with them, and then rolling them up in a towel and jumping on them a bit (Thanks Francis Cade for that tip). Then two sets of "normal people" clothes for hanging around and looking cool in Berlin □

- **A sleeping pad** tied to front fork with voile straps (these are "the best" lightweight straps for bikepacking. I will fight you on this. Physically.)

- A **Frame bag** with all the gubbins I might need. Tubes, pump, multi-tool, cable-ties, quicklinks, duct tape. Lights and spare lights. Powerbank (how the fudge do people exist in $currentYear without powerbanks?)

- **GPS cycle computer** (basically a fancy satnav). I imagine this makes bike touring 20x easier nowadays than in the old days. Imagine having to memorise or plot the 620 miles to Berlin with paper maps ☹.

- **Rucksack**...well that's technically on me, not the bike. Most cycle-trippers ride without a backpack. I agree it's nicer to just add an extra pannier bag. A backpack puts way more weight and strain on your shoulders and back (derrrr!!!!), the straps can dig into you, and it leads to way more back sweat. At the end of big trips my back looks like a pepperoni pizza! But I just carry a backpack everywhere because it's so convenient when off the bike? It's a hard habit to break. I "should" limit what I put in there, keep it light. But then you get baited into "well if I've got the space".

The rucksack carries important stuff you want easy access to like passport, money, headphones, raincoat...chocolate bars. Finally a chunky book on cell-biology which I'd been labouring to finish. Didn't read a single page on the whole trip. Ended up giving it away in a hostel in Berlin. ☐

Bicycle to Berlin: Pain in the Rain. Legs Slain. Little Gain. Should have gone to Spain….Instead.

To truly be a "*Bicycle to Berlin*", I should have started from my house in Canterbury and cycled the 20 miles to the Dover ferry terminal. If I'd known I'd be doing a write-up of the trip, and being judged by pernickety book-nerds...I probably would have done it. But cycling for a specific ferry is just unnecessary stress. There's a lot of hills on the way to Dover. I had no idea how long it was going to take on this ridiculous bike. And do you add on time to fix any punctures? I've cycled for a 7am checkin ferry before, and what ends up happening is you have to leave at about 5am. So then you've got to wake around 4am. After shite sleep, because you wake up every hour thinking "FUCK. IVE

MISSED MY ALARM AND…..oh no, don't worry, it's only 2am"…."FUCK I'v….3am"...etc.

So I'd spent the night round my parents and got a lift down to the port for first thing Tuesday morning. I had weird dreams. Significantly weirder than usual. Usually my dreams are incredibly mundane. I imagine other peoples dreams, yours, might be action-packed, Michael-Bay-esque, cinema-worthy epics. Not for me. I am usually planning on going somewhere interesting, but in the dream I get to the train station and the train is delayed. Typical. Further delays. Delays become cancellations. More cancellations. Eventually I end up waking just before my train finally arrives. The internet has told me these dreams indicate I'm either stressed or feeling unfulfilled, or stressed about feeling unfulfilled. I'm pretty sure my brain's just lazy. Very convenient for Mr Brain that he doesn't have to do any work rendering exotic landscapes. He can just keep me stuck at the train station, using minimal processing power and RAM. It's either that, or the dream is mirroring the realist side to my personality. It's simply an accurate portrayal of the British Transport System. Good band name that. Wonder if that's what BTS stands for. Doubt it.

But last night I didn't have that dream for once. Actually, this wasn't really a dream persay. More one of those groggy early-morning radical thoughts. Those brainwaves that feel like the most revolutionary and groundbreaking insight when they pop. Holy shit! This could change the world as we know it! Should i write it down? Nah I'm not gonna forget an idea so earth-shattering and special.....aaaaand by the time you're tucking into your toast...poof! It gone!

But this morning I actually scribbled it down. In hindsight they're never as great as they initially feel, but it's still interesting, and suggests I might have a future in product marketing if this whole software engineering thing goes tits up. Well it's probably not going to go tits up. But maybe I up my tits at it if my itch for a radical change grows too large. We are slowly creeping deeper and deeper into a dystopian present. Like a boiled frog. The melting Freddo of society. A present where Western societies are still making "progress", but what even is this progress? 99% of people seem slightly unhappier, everything you can buy has turned to shit and "*isn't built like it was used to*", and Freddo's are 30 pence. 30 pence! 30! pence! Back when I was given £1.50 a day for lunch money, I could buy 10 freddo's and still save 50p each day to go towards a Playstation 2. How the flip are kids meant to buy a PS5 these days?

Don't get me wrong, there's still some genuine progress, especially in medical fields. Which would be great, if the NHS hadn't been run into the ground by vultures eager to loot its corpse. Too much of this progress in recent years has been computerised. Saving us time or money. Increasing our efficiency. Keeping us entertained. Seeming good, but really just sapping our attention. Or robbing us of our autonomy and chance to think for ourselves. Turning us into a mere consumer; exploiting us to buy things we don't need, which don't actually improve our lives. We are entertained but unfulfilled. I entered Software thinking I could use my skills to improve the world. And whilst I haven't directly built these bullshit attention siphoning apps, I still feel guilty by association. My enjoyment and participation in building software feels like implicit endorsement. Endorsement of the direction society is trending. I could explain how my work does make people's lives better...I think. But it'd make this already overloaded paragraph unreadably long. What's an economy by the way? ¯_(ツ)_/¯ ...So when the robots rip out our bones for fuel, and teabag our still warm corpses; I can't help but feel complicit. Day-to-day, when I'm not thinking too hard, I still really enjoy computer programming, and I'm fortunate for it to fund all these silly adventures. Maybe that's the real issue. Just overthinking things a bit. Maybe it's better to just get on with it and savour the life we have. But is that just burying your head in the sand? Do we have an obligation and social responsibility to unheadsand ourselves?

…..Errr so anyway, I noted this early-morning idea down to remember it…also I went off on one a bit there. Sorry about that. I realise it's very early in the book to bring the mood crashing down. So it does get more lighthearted, trust me. Also maybe that passage is a bit cringey and a bit: "*Mate, you've been watching far too much fight club. Relax bro.*" But it's also a bit fucked that we don't seem to be able to acknowledge the sliding of society without it being cringey, lame, or like we're just trying to sound smart and sophisticated. Also things aren't black and white. It certainly doesn't seem like it so far, but I'm a pretty chill and happy person. We can enjoy life and still battle for a better one at the same time. Anyway…this early-morning-thought is well and truly over-hyped now. I've x-factor delayed the reveal for too long. But here it is:

Why spend big dosh enlisting athletes or minor celebrities to endorse your product? Who usually do so with incredible reluctance. Acting more wooden than my antique dildo collection. So why not use a historical figure instead, all for the paltry price of a wig and some makeup! Bargain. Examples:

Ragnarr Loðbrók: On the morning of a raid, I always remember to eat a hearty bowl of Shredded Wheat. It gives me the slow-release energy I need to pillage and plunder all morning long, without getting hangry. Ragnarr Loðbrók compels you:

1. Eat Shredded Wheat.
2. Shred the souls of the puny Englishmen.
3. Valhalla awaits you.

Boudica: When I'm on my period I can't just "*take a day off*" from rampaging through the armies of Rome. I need to be ready for battle at all times. That's why I use Always Super-Dry Maxi pads. They give me the confidence I need to disembowel my enemies every day. I know for sure that's not gonna be my blood on my thigh.

I fudging love the ferry companies. When I bought my tickets...I instantly realised I'd booked the wrong day, Monday not Tuesday. "*Fuck. Well that's £30 down the drain*". After dealings with airline and train companies; I know the immense pain after you "dare" to make a single, simple mistake on your ticket. "*Ooh, misspelt your name.*

Certainly we can change that for you sir...that'll just be £40'..."*Fuck off*". So in the queue for customer support I was practising my pleading voice. Whilst on hold I spotted the website lets you completely rebook your journey for free, no strings attached! (Eurostar has the same thing, but if you've realised it close to departure time, your ticket is probably now 4x the original price).

Train and airline companies also have a very heavy-handed policy with regards to explosive materials. Ferries are way more chill. I love GT-85. Comes in a shiny red, black and white spray-can. It is a water displacer, lubricant, and smells great! (bonus tip: Spray a little on your gloves pre-ride. If you start to struggle, give it a whiff and you'll feel all floaty and nice :) Cracking stuff*).

*note: don't actually do this. Or at least don't sue me when your lungs fall to pieces.

The only downside is it has a pretty explosive symbol on the packaging. When checking in for the ferry I saw a sign saying: "*Any goods with these symbols are prohibited*". One of those symbols is printed boldly on the side of the GT-85 can.

A half-asleep, bald, sturdy unit of a middle-aged man handed me back my passport and ticket.

"Oh, before I go; that symbol over there. I've got a big can in my bag with that on. Do I need to leave it here? I kind of need it for cleaning my bike?"

in a deep, bored voice: "....errr...just keep it in your bag then"

"Are you sure? It does say 'strictly prohibited'"

Frustrated: "Look mate. Do you want to catch this ferry or not?"

"Cheers. Guess I'll just keep it in my bag then."

It was a crisp, cool morning at Dover. A handful of other cyclists were making the trek across and were gathered in lane 81 chatting. My ridiculous stickered bike was looking a bit out of place compared to their professional setups. But I guess that kind of matches my scruffy look. Cheap fluorescent yellow pinnacle cycling top, no time for Rapha (technically no money for Rapha…well "technically technically" I've got some money, I'd just rather spend it on exquisite cheesecakes than spend it looking smart).

Unshaven, but not the handsome stubble you see in Gillette adverts, yet also not a proper beard. Instead perpetually in facial-hair limbo. Looking like I'm attempting to grow a beard…and failing. My messy brown hair flowing in the breeze. Immediately after I get a trim, I glance in the mirror and fancy myself as Aragorn from Lord of the Rings…well maybe not quite Aragorn, maybe a hot Boromir…but still not bad. Then I say thanks and leave, immediately strap on my helmet, and it never looks like that again until the next cut. On most days it takes a life of its own. Invariably ending up in some form of scraggly mad-scientist style, strands wisping off in every direction. I chain drink hot chocolates from the secret, cheap vending machine hidden by the toilet block. This lets me semi-avoid smalltalking with the other cyclists. Nothing against them, just not in the mood right then.

The ferry was super smooth. Whiled away the time chatting to a pair of nice cycling blokes from Yorkshire. Being in cycling gear on a ferry is a good social ice-breaker, even non-cycling people are often curious as to what you're doing, and where you're going.

The ferry breakfast hack: It's about £14, but the kids meal is less than half that price! I can pick only 4 items, rather than

8. But I still get a massive coffee with it. Bosh! I'm a failing vegetarian nowadays anyway, and limiting to 4 items makes it easier to avoid the temptations of the breakfast bacon, which always dominates the smell-market at the breakfast and is mouth-watering. You'll probably notice throughout this book I don't describe a single other smell. My sense of smell is pretty fucked. I can smell when something's died, or someone's just done a shit (or both at the same time like with Elvis. Although was he legally dead pre-shit? Not sure it matters as I've heard you empty your bowels on death, so dying on the toilet might be the most sensible place to do it. Well done Elvis :thumbs-up:). But apart from that…. :shrug: I don't think the low-level hay-fever helps. When you properly suffer from extreme hay-fever, it's very noticeable, so you use tablets to deal with it. For low-level sufferers like myself, you forget, but over 14 hours out in nature it adds up, and eventually your nose is as clogged as (**editor note**: insert disgusting metaphor here). I brought a pack of antihistamines with me. Never used one. Cannot explain why. Tangent: If you want to make big bucks, buy a bulk load of anti-histamines. Take them to botanical gardens. Walk around selling them at 10x markup. No idea why the gardens don't just sell them their-selves.

I was talking about the breakfast, you have to be a bit careful with the free coffee though. Pay before you pick up a mug. I once had a grumpy old french chap charge me for the kids meal and a separate coffee. Disaster. I get very irate if I look around the ferry restaurant. I cannot comprehend how someone can spend £14 on food, and then just not eat half of it. What in the fudge? Literally breaks my penny-pinching brain. So when I was feeling hard-done-by about being charged for the coffee, as the staff came around clearing up plates, when clearing my obviously clean plate...I asked if he was just going to bin the two sausages poking out of another family's plate. He was. Then could I have them?..."*erm, ok. Do you need your cutlery back?*" He'd already cleared my stuff. I didn't want to make life awkward for him after my already weird food-minesweeping request: "Nah, I like to just dunk them in my coffee anyway!". I was confused and surprised at the words that had just escaped my mouth. But now I was committed, so I grabbed the two sausages by hand. Dunked them. Chomped them. Was surprisingly actually quite nice. Recommend it.

The ferry ride was dry, with hints of sunshine. The industrial complex of Dunkerque being slightly less poignant and impressive than the majestic white cliffs...but like a greyhound in the traps, I am still raring to go and licking my fingers at what's ahead.

I've already eaten half of my special sandwiches from boredom whilst the ferry finally pulls in (peanut-butter and honey; and cranberries; and walnuts; and maybe some protein powder; and maybe creatine monohydrate). The Dunkerque journey is weird. It bombs along the channel. Then just goes agonisingly sideways along the coast for 40 minutes.

Dark clouds form as we roll off the ferry, it starts spitting with rain. One of the Yorkshiremen (Yorkies?) claimed the forecast was intermittent showers. But it does not stop spitting with rain....For 6 hours. Flipping Belgium. Miserable weather, even in the last week of May, which should theoretically be summer.

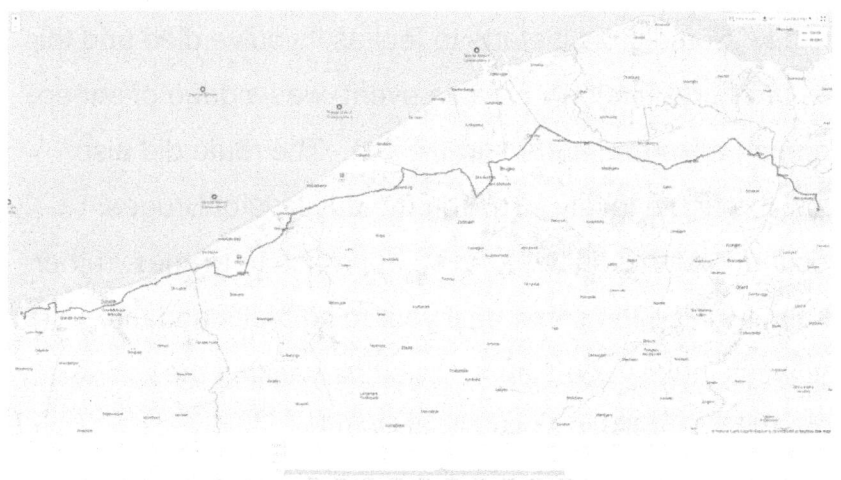

I was heading East. The fastest route out of France possible, into northern Belgium. Still East, then cutting south around Ghent. To hopefully camp somewhere south of Ghent for the evening. About 70 or 80 miles, not as much as I'd need to ride each day, but by the time you're off the ferry, you've lost an hour to the timezones, so it's nearly 12 when you start.

Northern Belgium is pretty boring once you've done it several times. The cycling infrastructure is great for getting around. But it is just flat, fairly lifeless farmland and canals. I prefer bustier countries. Don't get me wrong. It's nicer to be out in the countryside than the city. But with no cars trying to knock you off the road, no hills to test your lungs and legs, no potholes to destroy your bike and rearend....not even corners. Just a flat, empty cyclepath, stretching out to infinity. Sometimes it starts to feel as if you've died and this is purgatory. The only notable event was a gang of sheep, forming a North Flanders traffic jam. The route did also flow through a lovely forest on the outskirts of Bruges. I recommend this as the "nicest" approach to Bruges, rather than following the canal until your mind melts and the dullness makes you start envisioning yanking the handlebars and just steering straight in.

Bruges is a very pretty city. Highly recommend day/weekend-tripping it from South England if you live close to Dover/channel-tunnel. It's filled with quaint old buildings and streets. But….I've been to Bruges about 14 times in the past couple of years. I almost always pass through it en-route to the Netherlands (I go there a couple of times a year due to their friendly legal policy on magic mushrooms...plus it's just a nice, relaxing cycling country). So this time I just do a quick stop at the fanciest, massive church from **In Bruges**. And say to myself: "Hey, I'm in Bruges. Like the film, **In Bruges**". I still chuckle, and wonder when that joke will finally get old. And I'm off again. "Hey, weren't you complaining about the dull Belgian countryside being monotonous...and then you are in one of the most beautiful cities in Europe and you don't even stop for a coffee. And to cherry the top you then looped around and avoided Ghent, another stunning city?".....Yes….your point?

The rain would not be stopped. I was still in shorts and short-sleeved top. I've got a raincoat, but I never use it even in the pouring rain. Turns you into a boil-in-a-bag cyclist. So the only use for it is looking fly in the club when the Euro-techno comes on. The luminescent strips really pop! When the rain picked up, there would be parts of the route where I wouldn't see another cyclist or pedestrian for miles. It's a very strange feeling to cycle past a country, family house. The kitchen window a beacon of light in the dark, grey Belgian afternoon. You see a lovely family sitting down to a lavish dinner. All warm and smiling. While I'm out here, in the pissing wind and rain. Wet to the bone. On a stupid fucking looking bike, with done-zo legs. "Why can't I just let myself be happy and content like them?" "Why do I have to always be doing some ridiculous shit?" "And for what reason anyway? I wonder if other amateur wannabe-athletes have these questions and doubts? Why do I invest so much energy into brutalising my body? If I directed this energy elsewhere, couldn't I make the world such a better place? Make people happy? Maybe it is the way that meaningful change of our current social systems feels so impossible or implausible, that we have to direct our energies elsewhere. If it was 100 years ago, I would be using this energy to free the profiteroles from their predicament. Or 300 years ago, toppling kings to free the prawns. Instead I'm losing my mind and singing: "*The legs on the man go round and round...round and round...round and round*" three-hundred times in a row to my saturated self.

(**note to editor**: Maybe remove the above? Re-reading it feels a little too cringey. Like I'm """"subtly"""" hinting that I could overthrow the establishment if I could be bothered. So Subtle. I respect walking the walk, not talking the talk. And here I am not a walker. It's like that person who claims: "Bro, I could have a 6-pack if I just stopped eating cheesecakes and beasted the gym at 5am every morning!"....yeah, but you're fucking not gonna are you? Soo...... ¯_(ツ)_/¯. But maybe it should be left, I don't want to shy away from my embarrassing, deluded musings. [**editor note**: ...... fuck it ._.])

Oh yeah. The wind :) It wasn't a massive headwind, and at times was just a cross-headwind. But this bike was not designed for aerodynamics. My legs felt like they were pushing hard, but I was just crawling. Couldn't get above 15mph.

It's not just my legs that have problems. The plasters on my thumb keep coming off and need replacing. Getting mud and crud sprayed into open wounds can't be good. The day before my trip I'd been cooking my pre-holiday speciality: "everything left in my fridge with rice". I'd had a minor mishap. I believe the term is target fixation? The same thing that leads drunk people to crash into static objects, which seem very easy to avoid crashing into. As I was slicing and dicing I thought to myself: "It sure would be inconvenient if I accidentally sliced my finger off the day before leaving. Boy, I'd better be careful". Sure enough, 3 seconds later...and the blade is in my thumb. For a normal human they'd probably have lopped off the whole thumb. But fortunately, experts have informed me that I have such a superior reaction time, that I could be a formula 1 driver or a fighter pilot. I just choose not too, because chicks go crazy for a man in Business-to-Business Trade Credit Solutions Software Engineering. So I was capable of pulling away before the knife drove too deep to require hospital trips. But it's still a pain, especially in the rain. I'm sure "waterproof" plasters are a scam. Any plaster I place is flapping about in the wind within an hour.

I close in on a campsite around Wachtebeke, on the Dutch-Belgian border just north of Ghent, around 7pm. Thoughts of cycling through the night and getting to Germany in a single ride seem laughable now. This is what I'd been thinking of on the ferry. Maybe I could just bomb it to Germany, no stops. Gogogo. I shake my head as I think about how deluded I can be sometimes...although is it delusion. On a better leg day, with the right weather, that probably would have happened. The campsite reception is proper closed. Quell surpris. Fortunately when I dial the number the "ranger/warden", a tall, gangly man comes over in a pickup truck and says I can stay and pay when it opens tomorrow.

Things are looking up. 13€ for a campsite with free hot showers. Mental.

At the campsite I simply shower, plan for tomorrow and try and get an earlyish night. There's a lot of time to think on boring Belgian cyclepaths, and even more time when you're camping on a seemingly deserted Belgian campsite, no-one else around. A lot of my thinking through the day had been about some woman I know. I'll give her a pseudo-name to keep it anonymous....Gary. Although Gary, if you're reading this, I've also not put in any dodgy details or anything personal just in-case, because I do quite like Gary as a person, and I'm a pretty paranoid and cautious person....am

I cautious? I'm cautious when events can have negative consequences for others...but when they only have negative consequences for me...it's full steam ahead! All aboard The Fucking Myself Up train!

Anyway, r.e. Gary. I always thought with life that there's a Venn diagram for partners' attributes. And you're inevitably going to have to decide which sectors are more important to you, and which you can live without. Life is full of compromises. But it felt like this was somehow a person that resided in the intersection of: funny and a great laugh, not a neo-nazi, kind and considerate, breathtakingly beautiful, intelligent, not committing philosophical suicide (This ones a bit odd, but it's from Camus who said: "*philosophical suicide is the unwillingness to grapple with the very nature of life, and by this, never "truly live.""*. I struggle to have deep relationships with people who shy away from the darker side of life and existence. I worry that I'm going to say something that lifts the veil and just ruins their life. This sounds a bit pompous, I don't expect this to happen in most cases, but even with low probability I don't want to risk it. A bit like how life felt really simple for me when I just trusted what my brain thought and believed it never lied to me. It becomes a tad time-consuming with every rationalisation becoming: "*Do I truly think that? Or is my brain just lying to me because it doesn't want to admit it's scared to look foolish*").

Somehow Gary fits in this tiny intersection of Venn. She has it all, although….she is a mouse-murderer. Hmmm. I reckon I overlook that because: What in the flip are you gonna do with a "humanely" caught mouse in London. Drive to the Chilterns at 3am to set him free? And then she gets a pass because of meeting all the other bullet points. Hopefully not the beautiful one. I don't want to give people free-passes from their looks. If anything, I've heard about how good-looking people get treated nicer, and I try to deliberately counteract that. A couple of my friends are probably reading that and thinking: "*hmmm...so if it seems like he's especially nice to me…..wait a minute!*" But yeah, can't hide from the fact that she is just the kind of person who lights up a room, like everyone else is in black and white, and she's draped in neon, like someone going as Hong Kong for Halloween to a funeral….nice, I'm gonna do that next year. That or a Neon Nazi. The costume, not the funeral.

Holy tangent batman, so back on track, yeah Gary. I was a fan.
We do also have quite different interests, she is deathly afraid of my two main hobbies: cycling and climbing. And I

have never been to a play in my life. Or have I? Are those the "HE'S BEHIND YOU!" things. Maybe I have then. Clearly a man of culture.

So we do have many differences, but when you've got a crush on someone, your brain downplays the differences, whilst simultaneously amping up the things you do share. Anyway it's good to have *some* distinct hobbies in relationships. Gives each of you a bit of space. Saves you from the: *"Please just leave me alone for 10 minutes. I don't care what you do. Where you go. Just be not around me for every single microsecond of existence. ARGRRGHHHH!"*. No idea why I'm speaking like an authority here. In my thirties and never had a "proper" relationship in my life. Some expert. I slightly blame the *"just be yourself"* advice-givers here though. And then you describe to them what *"just being yourself"* on a first date entails. For instance, maybe you tell them about your alliance with the spiders. *"Well OK, obviously not like that"*. Right....so just be myself, but don't express any sides of my personality that make me myself.

"Yeah, now you're getting it. Just do that!" :) So I'm no relationship guru, although I have watched every episode of Seinfeld...twice!

And the simulations I had run so far were coming back good. I'm a very independent person and usually if you're doing something I'm not into I'll say: "This isn't my cuppa tea. I'm gonna head off and do something fun. Rather than this. Which is shit and lame. Cya". But she might be one of the few people where I'd actually rather do shite things together, over cool things by myself. Well not shite things, she'd make the shite bearable. Unshite. Although I could potentially do non-shite things with a non-shite person. Hmmm. I'm really not selling this well, even to myself. Maybe it was just a crush and I get carried away.

But did Gary like me back? I mean I knew Gary liked me, we got on great whenever we were together at group stuff. We laughed a lot. I'm pretty sure that deep-down we're both people who crave creativity but are "stuck" in sensible places in our lives. Comfortable well paying jobs with nice colleagues. Like a warm bed on a winter morning, tough to throw off the sheets, bin the career and loudly proclaim: "*I SHALL BECOME AN ARTIST!!!....now then, where do I apply for the money from being an artist?....Oh....Well then how do I eat food to live?.....Oh*". But from her side, was it "like", or "like like"? Argggg, these questions, plus simulations of life if it transpired to be "like like", all these things were going through my mind a lot. Not knowing was driving me to madness. But I've never been adept at untangling romantic signals. It feels like that part of my brain got forgotten whilst under construction, like a bodged new-build: "*whoops did you need level floors?*". There's a cornucopia of face-palm inducing memories from my past to pick from, but these are just the two most egregious examples:

Example 1:
- Hey, there's only 1 bed. You should sleep in the bed with me.
- Nah it's alright, you take the bed.
- I think you should DEFINITELY sleep in the bed with me.
- …….Nah :)
- hmmmm :|
- Don't worry. I've got an inflatable double-mattress. I did buy the cheapest foot-pump in Go Outdoors though, so it's gonna take about 30 minutes to blow-up. But I don't mind.
- Maybe I can help with the blowing.
- No, I can blow it myself just fine. But thanks for offering.

I added the last two lines. But the first lines are genuine.

Example 2:
- Do you want to come in for a coffee

- At this hour? Do you realise that caffeine has a half-life of 6 hours? I guess not based on that wild suggestion!

- Welllll, maybe we wouldn't be doing much sleeping ;)

- Hmmmmm....That's actually really unhealthy. I've just finished reading "*Why We Sleep: The New Science of Sleep and Dreams*". Missing out on quality sleep will take days of your lifespan.

- (grumpy tone): OK. Thanks. I'll give that a read. Good night then. :|

So yeah when it comes to romance I end up a blundering bull in a Chinese takeaway. Chow-mein everywhere. No subtlety. No suave. The anti-bond. "*The name's Johnny. Johnny Knight. Would you like to have fuck with me?*" So when there's people in my life who I'm thinking: "*They're alright. Attractive. Not a neo-nazi*", it's usually not worth me bumbling around and risking soiling the existing relationship equilibrium. But Gary was different. There's only 3 people in my life (now 4) who I've felt strongly enough about (in a romantic sense), that it actually caused me anguish and yearning. And it'd been years since my last good yearn. So especially with the tough first day, a large part of me just wanted the trip to be over and done; just leap forward a week in time. I was just counting down the time until I could ask if she wanted to go out, have a bit of closure on the "like" vs "like-like". Even if it's just "like", at least I can move-on from massively overthinking about Gary, and back to massively overthinking about the most effective way to deal with creep spread in Terran vs Zerg (Starcraft stuff. I'm still doing Hellion-Banshee openings like it's 2016. Hello, the past called. They want their build-orders back!).

Bicycle to Berlin: Day 2. Problems Anew.

...13 euro for 2 hours of broken as fuck sleep. The deal is looking a little less hot. It was the most obnoxious weather you can get whilst camping. Not steady rain. But bursts of heavy showers. Loud enough to wake you up. Not consistent enough for your brain to adjust, filter and sleep through. (Yeah yeah, I should have brought earplugs. I'm an effing moron. Eff you ;))

Extremely frustrating start to day 2:
The plan is to be deep into Germany by the end of day 2, but I'm still in Belgium. Nowhere close. I have to wait around until reception opens at 9am to pay for the night. And of course the booking software shits the bed when we try to book me in for a date in the past. Every time we stumble past one cryptic error, we hit another. It's like being at work. So 30 mins later I simply pay in cash, then walk off leaving her to deal with it.

Id accidentally left my bonephones* on all night, so I had nothing to listen to on the final mind-numbing Belgian cyclepaths to infinity.

* Bone-conduction headphones. They loop **over** your ears and the vibrations play the music into your ears without blocking them. My review:
- For music: shite. A £150 pair sounds like a £5 pair.
- Podcasts or audiobooks: Absolutely fine.
    - On this trip I'd been listening off and on to a book about ultra-processed food, pretty apt as I'm smashing nutrition bars full of ultra-processed ingredients.
    - They're also nice in the office, you can eavesdrop on office conversations and gossip. If it's fun you can pause the bonies and join in. If it's boring you turn up the bonies and ignore it.
    - Plus you can't really put a price on the safety and convenience (well I guess you can, it's one-fifty big ones). Note: It's still less safe than not listening to anything at all. I still pause them when coming up to awkward junctions.

Then I need to pick up food for the day from the nearby town (Wachtebeke). I'd heard that Aldi on the continent is actually really good.....it's not. It's dogshit. Shite bakery section for Belgium*. And I doubt a vegetarian has ever stepped foot in there judging by sandwich selection. Everything in single use plastic...

*Tangent: Belgian bakeries best bakeries. The main thing that disappointed me about Paris was the patisseries. Everything in them looks divine....but then it just tastes....alright. Don't tease me like that Paris patisseries 😣.

It's style over substance. Strongly against my philosophy. Belgian bakery stuff looks pretty plain, but tastes god-tier. Chocolate and vanilla cream in a "pain au"...genius. Although I do feel the humble Reisstartje has a lot of untapped potential. You've got a great base there, just some chopped nuts or drizzled melted chocolate could really push it over the edge into the king of baked goods imo. If you know anyone who works at Panos please pass this on.

Tangent 2 (**editor note**: dear god. This can't be readable): I know it's virtually impossible to fully cut out single use plastic. But can try my best. You also discover your diet improves massively through trying to avoid it. Cuts out the one-off snacks. Note: heavy emphasis on the word "try". Lower emphasis on the word "best"!

Then when I've finally picked out my basket of food, my eyes flick to the checkouts. FFS. It's just like UK Aldi*. Single lane open. Several large trollies waiting. I don't have an hour to waste. So I huff and stomp back around the supermarket, putting back what I've got. Next I must hurdle the alarm gate on one of the closed checkouts to actually be able to leave. Argh.

*Since this trip my local UK Aldi has installed self-checkout machines. After raging against the machine earlier, I should be appalled by this……but not having to spend so long queueing is quite nice. Ideally hire more people, but then I guess you get what you pay for.

Went to Delhaize on the other side of town. Flippin' love Delhaize. Beautiful baguettes. Great nuts. Top-notch bakery. I feel a little bad for the people of Wachtebeke though. What remained of the bakery section resembled Lindisfarne monastery after the Vikings were through with it. Absolutely ransacked.

Bakery raided, ready to go? Not on your Nelly*! Turns out I'd actually been at "the wrong campsite". My planned day 2 route started from a campsite 12 miles further south. So yet more faffing about getting an updated route onto the cycle computer, and the severely optimistic 200mile route to get me into Germany was lagging and crashing it, so I needed to split that into sections. Sigh. I. Just. Want. To. Ride. My. Bike.

*Nelly interlude:
It's getting hot in here. So hot. So take off all your clothes....
"No Nelly, I'm not gonna do that. Why don't you just turn down the fucking thermostat? ITS THE MIDDLE OF FUCKING NOVEMBER! What's your flipping problem dude? Haven't you been paying attention to the whole climate change thing? I know we split the bills, but this is taking the fucking piss. If I find either of these two fucking gigantic space heaters on again, I'm done. They're going in the bin and you're footing the whole bill! FUCKING SORT IT OUT NELLY! Jeez."

Alright no more interludes or tangents for a while. This is taking the piss now.

By the time I could "actually" claim I was cycling in the Berlin direction...it was 11:45. And it had started raining. Brilliant. Brilliant Belgium

The second day in a row my legs felt weak. I was struggling 40 miles in. It was dawning on me that over 100 miles a day, on such a turd of a bike, may have been nibbling off more than my legs could chew.

Positive news: Remembered that I have blister plasters, which actually do stay on, whatever the weather. So I made the renegade move of using a blister plaster on a non-blister cut. Rules? I don't play by them 😎

It took until the late afternoon to notice my groin was on fire. Like a boiled frog. This is not good. Legs yelling at you can be ignored. Or at least silenced with sugar. Nether regions yelling at you cannot be placated. On big rides, things can go down south down south very rapidly. Apologies for those thinking it would be nice to have a quick read whilst on lunch break, or with their breakfast. But we must address the grim reality of what goes on in my underwear. Cycling turns the area into a wet, swampy sweat box. This is the dream destination for a bacterial holiday. And my groin was Costa del Sol. Any skin problems that commence down there need treating with utmost seriousness. If you keep riding, extra chafing means things can only get worse. And when the skin is breached, the bacterial holiday zone makes infection common. If you're young and fit you probably think yourself pretty invincible. But infection and septicaemia can be deadly whatever your age.

I'd already been silly and not addressed my groin early enough. The easiest way to cover the most distance is actually by minimising stops rather than going faster. This makes it easy to fall into a trap where you get sunburnt, or nearly piss yourself, just to optimise doing everything in one stop. Professionals can do both (pee and suncream) mid-ride, but the embarrassment of having to explain why I ended up in a canal or hedge, means I've never quite perfected this trick. If you're looking for dong on daytime TV, watching the early footage of grand tour races is a real treat. You usually get a decent second or two before the cameraman realises what is happening, then panic-pans 180 degrees to the roadside-scenery.

So earlier on I'd been thinking: "I'll have a look at that when I need to pee". But I didn't need to pee. Eventually the discomfort reached the level where I was doing "the ministry of silly cycles" just to search for positions that minimised the fire in my loins. Slowing me down yet further. When I finally said "enough is enough", stopped and had a pervy peek down my shorts...uh-oh, my inner things were fiery red. Uh-oh. Being so behind I can't just stop though, so I hope for "better late than never", place a big blister plaster on the inside of each leg and pray.

Despite the groin gremlins, my mood is better than yesterday. I am out of the Belgian roads I have seen too many times before. I'm out into the unknown. Buoyed by the sense of exploration. Seeing places and things I have never seen before. It is hard to put the sense of exploration into words. You don't really notice "Oh. I am exploring. This is enjoyable". It is just an invisible hand that pushes your general mood and optimism up. Guess this is why people enjoy travel, so it's not really restricted to cycling. Didn't even need my bonies in the end. Simply enjoying my eyes seeing new things.

Another positive: For a "Summer" adventure, I am saving an awful lot of money on sunscreen. And the weather is better than yesterday, still grey. But mainly dry and grey. Any showers are actual showers. Not the bullshit from yesterday.

I snap a quick selfie as I tick visiting Boom off my "funny place name" bucket list. Boom is just below Antwerp. Just a shame I didn't have time to hunt around for a "Welcome to Boom" sign. There's also a Grobbendonk next door 😊

Sat on a bee.

I'm finally into Southern Netherlands, Limburg. It is where Netherlands is pretty thin, so I should be able to make Germany today...sort of on schedule. Realistic schedule that is. Not the initially way over-ambitious "I'm gonna ride all night. Because I'm Mr Hardcore. Yeah Buddy! Ride and/or die!" schedule.

I'm cycling through the small town of Strampoy around 6:30pm. The sun….yes I said the sun! First time on the trip…..the sun is setting, and it's a nice evening. Things are looking up! But I am running low on food and water. And I have no idea what will happen tonight. I have nothing booked. Will I be able to rock up late at a campsite again, will I hotel it? Either way it might be too late to get food on arrival. So I double-back into Strampoy and stop at the big yellow Jumbo supermarket.

Sorry if this book seems to just be me complaining about rain, my legs and my groin in that specific order....but that's cycle-tripping! In hindsight I expect my legs were just weak and I was tired, but whilst shopping in Jumbo I'd convinced myself the chain was the problem. It clearly needed cleaning and lubricating. Then I'd be flying right?

As Dutch people go about their daily shopping I clean and lube the chain in the parking lot. The shoppers pass me by without a care. Apart from one animated old Dutch man with raggedy hair. The kind of person who might be homeless, but you're not sure, and it would be a bit insulting to assume so. A bit like my current look to be honest, so I am one to talk eh xD. He seems very interested in the "Fietser". But "Sprek oo engels" is greeted with a friendly laugh but a "no". So I explain "Ik sprek geen Nederlands". This doesn't stop him from continuing to speak Dutch, I can only shrug.

When I'm finishing the cleaning, my eyes pass over the cassette, laughing again at how crooked and dodgy the teeth look. Pretty sure this bike is just built from all the pieces that fail quality control somewhere. Errrrrr....isn't there supposed to be a bolt there? The bolt whose sole purpose is to keep the back wheel attached to the frame.

It's nowhere to be found. I look around on the ground. Nothing. This is a problem. It is fairly important for a bicycle that the rear wheel stays attached. Fortunately it had not come off yet. I guess because gravity sort of kept it in place. But a big jolt from a pothole or bump could send it flying off at any time. If this happened down a big hill…the trip was over, and that was best case scenario! It is really a testament to the quality of Belgian and Dutch cycle-paths that it had not already come flying off. It would not have lasted 10 minutes down the country lanes around Canterbury.

The friendly geezer says something which sounds like "all good". I shake my head and point to the missing bolt. This starts a frustrating 15 minute "conversation". He speaks Dutch louder. I speak English louder. He waves his arms. I wave my arms. I open the translate app on my phone. He doesn't seem interested. He beckons me to follow him. Well, I'm not going anywhere in a hurry without a secured rear-wheel, so why not?

He leads me to a local bike shop, which had agonisingly closed 10 minutes earlier. But at least the town has one! Then on google maps I find there's a campsite on the outskirts of town. Overall not the worst place to discover the bike is falling apart. I try to tell the man my plan: I'm just going to stay at the campsite and go back to the bike-shop tomorrow morning. Another 15 minutes of me yelling "Campsite" and him yelling "Ja......<something something> fietser"...it finally clicks. Maybe the campsite would have a spare bolt! Turns out yelling louder and waving your arms sometimes actually does help!

Rock up to the campsite around 7pm. No-one to be found. This isn't a big campsite. In fact it just seems to be someone's garden. I had nowhere else to (safely) go, so I sit and wait. A fellow camper informs me that the family running it are usually out until around 8pm.

When they come back a thin-bearded friendly looking chap greets me and says "of course I could stay". I explain the bike and we go to his impressive toolshed filled with bits and bobs. I'm not really one for gender roles, but it does feel a little emasculating when you have the DIY skills of a lemon, and your home toolset consists of a single screwdriver and pliers.....then you see a real man's garage. Wow. Despite the impressive array of nuts, bolts and tools....he doesn't have the correct bolt for the bike. He also gets the neighbour round who confirms the thread-size means it was a bike specific bolt, so it's not common and it'll definitely need a bike-shop. Should be disappointing, as it means I have to wait until the bike-shop opens at 9am, but I'd never realistically expected the campsite could sort it.

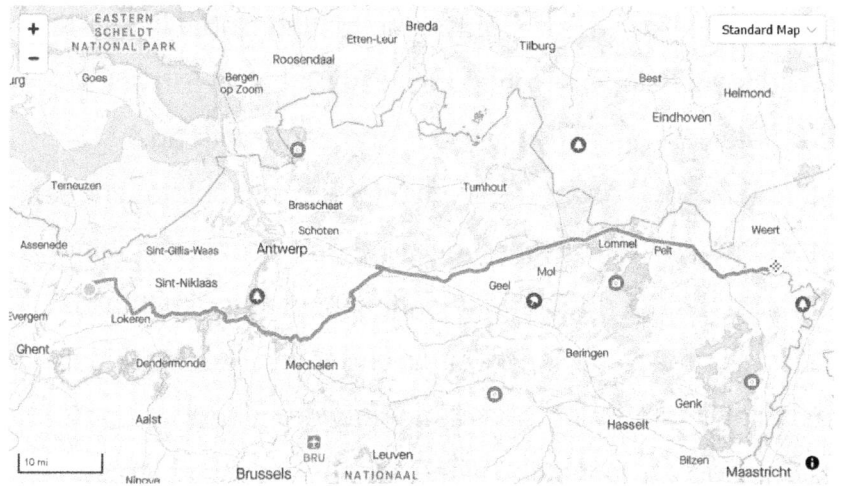

I'd been the consummate professional whilst journeying through Belgium. I'd resisted the tantalising temptations of the holy Belgian trinity. Belgian fries. Belgian waffles. And most importantly Belgian Beer. I'm not much of a beerie, but Belgian beer is the tits. It will also knock you for six if you're not careful. Often double the percentage of regular beer.

So it was a bit risky to join the campsite Belgian beer tasting evening adventure, especially when I was so far behind schedule and with a broken bike. But fuck it. If I'm going to fail, might as well have a good time whilst failing xD.

This wasn't like your haughty wine tasting club. No spit buckets, just sick buckets. Lads! LADS! L A D S!!! Joke: fortunately it was fairly civilised. And came with an interesting food assortment: cucumbers, chocolate, cheese, salad and crisps...all together, piled on top of one another, bit weird. I did a double-take on first seeing it, but it tasted delicious and made for great picking food. The breakfast the following morning was also pretty crazy and ostentatious. Looked like what you see royalty being served in period dramas. Fruit and cheese overflowing platters.

Big cheers to the campsite owners, and the inhabitants (a group of home-schooling families). We had a great time. They seemed impressed and excited about the challenge. One guy suggested I could vlog it. e.g. Some famous Dutch person was doing some other cycling thing, and they were vlogging it, and that was good. I agree that some people would watch it, and find it interesting. The problem I have with doing that is authenticity. How can anyone behave authentically when they have a camera on them? Would somebody ever be brazen enough to start a conversation thread with "*How about them immigrants eh?*" if they're being recorded. It's the same for me (or you). If you are recording yourself are you truly authentic? With this book I'm trying to be as authentic as possible. And I know things can be omitted, exaggerated, or even plain fabricated. But that's only the book that's fucked. At least my original experience was not tainted by me or others acting inauthenticly.

I did feel a little bad that I was the lone Englishman, so it kind of forced the group to avoid speaking in their native language. Some of them just did speak to each other in Dutch, which I was happy with. But an overly kind person tried to keep shifting the conversation into English to include me, which was nice and well-intentioned, but I'd rather have not intruded and let them have at it in Dutch. I definitely feel guilty about having English first language privileges. Just not enough to actually do anything about it and learn a 2nd language. If I was to learn a 2nd language, Dutch would be where I visit the most, but in a way not knowing Dutch makes the trips more relaxing and holiday-like. When you're walking around, or eating alone, your brain automatically eavesdrops and makes it hard to get into a chill, zen zone. But people warbling in a funny sounding language cannot be eavesdropped. There's something really relaxing about hearing Dutch being spoken. Whilst we're on language-guilt…as someone who is not comedian-level funny, but a fairly funny guy, and gets dopamine hits from making people laugh at parties or gatherings…I also feel a little guilty. Because being quick-witted in a second language, which your brain is chugging to parse, seems orders of magnitude harder. So I imagine non-native english people who might come across as a bit dull to me, could be the life of the party and absolute legends in their main tongue.

Anyway, the night was winding down. I wanted to thank the hosts for their incredible generosity. So I got out my pushbike, said "watch this", and did a perfect double-backflip over one of the picnic tables.

(**editor note**: What? What in the fuck is this? Even I was confused to find this mini paragraph on re-read/second draft. If this is left in, you can tell I've been told I need to hit a specific word-count. [**note from editor**: 70k Baby. WOOOOOOO!!!])

If you get up in the middle of the night to pee. And when you come back to your tent a black cat sprints out of it and into the undergrowth...is that good or bad luck? I didn't find a poo...so I'm going with good luck.

Bicycle to Berlin: Day 3, This Day is Key.

Got to bike shop for 9am. Keen. Nervous. Would they have a replacement bolt? Wheeled it round to the spacious workshop in back. The workshop had lots of tools in and was the size of two rooms. Can't remember what size room. There was a couple of men who I can't describe, because I've forgotten what they look like. Apologies to them, not saying they were forgettable, I was just worried and focussed on the bike. Only really looking at the hands of the guy who helped. Big hands? One of them might have had a moustache. Or might not. (**note to editor**: There's your "mental picture" of the place, happy now?).
Anywho...my heart sank when the first two bolts he fetched would not fit. Maybe European and English bikes have different standards? But my eyes lit up when the 3rd bolt looked identical to the missing one. It fit. Like Cinderella. Or goldilocks. I was as happy as either of them (editor note: did the bears not eat goldilocks? If not, why not?).

I was rolling by 9am. I could feel today was going to be a big day. Behind schedule, but when the chips are down, I bring the mother-flipping ketchup. I'd actually been looking at the ingredients of tomato ketchup whilst staying at my parents. For some reason whenever they go to burger king, or another fast food joint, my dad steals (he says "takes", but it's basically theft) about 10 ketchup packets. But they never seem to eat them. So there's just a big box filled with a couple of hundred outdated and rancid ketchup and BBQ sauce sachets. Oh, also sugar sachets stolen from coffee shops. Why?....Why? Back to the point, ketchup is basically just sugars, no fat, a little protein and salt......isn't that exactly what these expensive elite athlete performance drinks are? Tomato ketchup could well be the ultimate fuel for ultra-endurance athletes. I expect to see the next Tour de France full of riders squeezing ketchup bottles straight down their gullet.

Back to the original point before the tangent to the tangent....I was feeling mother-effing good. Optimistic and full of energy. Focussed. Eyes like a leopard. Stalking its prey. My prey being Berlin*. Me being the leopard. The eyes being mine.

* note: This is just a metaphor. I was not going to prey on the city of Berlin or its inhabitants. I am not a predator, sexual or otherwise.

I'm happy with my groin. Seems like the blister plasters have been doing the job. I believe the problem has been caused by the "comfortable" saddle on the granny-bike. It is made extra wide...for extra comfort? But this just leads to the nose being too fat, and grating my inner thighs on every pedal stroke.

Crossed the border to Germany in the woods outside Venlo (famous for its stuttering football club VVV Venlo) at almost exactly midday. Managed to ride in a big circle around Venlo after missing a turning, but it was a very nice circle through the woods. It was the first time I felt like I was making good progress. No morning bullshit to deal with. Just solid miles in the bank. Part of the swanky breakfast had been just massive blocks of cheese, so I polished off one of these as a reward for penetrating Germany.

It had been around 230 miles to the German border, but still over 400 miles to go, and nearly all the hills would come in the German part. So it was looking tough considering this was already the 3rd day of cycling. As I rode into the

German industrial heartland* it was "All gas, no breaks. Fuck Kitkats".

Well there was one break, and that was a disaster. Stopped in Mulheim. There were 2 foody coffee shops 50 yards apart. One looked super busy and popular. The other was dead.

So I did the sensible thing and went to the dead one. Why?

- A) You'll get served quicker. I'll probably hammer this point home multiple times, but you want to keep stops brief to avoid your body going too into recovery mode.

- B) often the empty places are perfectly fine, but people don't want to eat somewhere empty. But if no-one wants to eat at an empty place....you start to see the problem? So you can break the vicious cycle! If you sit outside and get something that looks amazing, like a waffle with all the trimmings....then by the time you finish, the place is heaving. Maybe it's just coincidence, but I believe in it and it makes me feel good to yell "I AM THE CATALYST MOTHERFUCKER!" (In my head of course [although no reason you couldn't do it out loud.....try it and let me know how it goes]).

The plan was a quick **"splash and dash"** (note: in this context I mean eating the food and drink very quickly, like a Formula 1 pit-stop. I am not referencing the other "splash and dash" context, where you use a restaurant bathroom to do number 2, then run off without actually purchasing anything). What a disaster. Ordered a simple coke +americano + scrambled eggs and some mozzarella & tomatoes on toast....14 euros. Outrageous. Daylight clobbery. But whatever...

"We'll bring it out for you"

So I wait on the table outside and start looking at maps. Remember dear reader, the place is dead. Yet 20 minutes later I'm still waiting. Literally nothing brought out. I go in to ask "Please can I have my coke zero now?"

"Oh yes, I'm so sorry. Here you go."

Drink the coke zero. 10 more minutes. Head back in again and politely ask for my coffee.

"Oh I'm so sorry, we are stressed. Sorry. Here".

Stressed about what, the zero other customers to deal with? Although I guess the non-existent source of customers would be stressful?

"Also I'll go check your food in the kitchen"

5 minutes later the food arrives. Finally.

A gust of wind immediately blows half the toppings onto the floor. Beyond caring. Eat with my bare hands like a wild animal. Egg was good.

Staff were super friendly, just completely away with the faeries!

Dark, looming clouds threatened me. It felt very much "once more into the breach" cycling towards this darkness. But thankfully they held their rain for the most part. Just a brief downpour today.

Went through Moers, crossed the Rhine on the outskirts of Duisburg, Essen, Bochum, Dortmund. All kind of blended into one. Felt like Medway or the London sprawl, where you've supposedly left one place and entered another, but there was no gap. Just suddenly the houses or buildings stopped being in X and started being in Y. The cities were as grey as the sky. The traffic lights were obnoxious. Having to get a 25kg bike up to speed from a dead-stop takes its toll. I would not recommend Dortmund as a holiday destination. Maybe it's fine, and maybe the opinion you get from one short cycle through a city can never be accurate. But just felt dodgy, run-down, unwelcoming. Men with dodgy dogs. Everything tagged without any artistic graffiti.

This was always going to be the "meh" part of the route anyway. But necessary if you want a fairly direct route to Berlin. You could skirt above the industrial heartland, but it would add a significant number of miles. It wasn't all bad, there was a fairly nice non-road, pure cyclepath through a large section of it. Many miles. And a weird barbed-wire building covered in spidermen...3 dimensional spidermen, not just pictures of spidermen....email me with how many you can spot in the picture (on the next page) for a chance to win fuck all! :)

I was slowly but surely adapting to the bike. Together we'd concocted a new radical riding style. A twist on the illegal* puppy-paws pose, but on this bike the diagonally facing bars actually made it safer than regular puppy-paws. You could rest most of your forearms on them and stay pretty stable. This combined with pushing my backside slightly off the end of the seat led to a position that was not only surprisingly aerodynamic, but also didn't cause as much arm and upper body ache as "going aero" on a proper road bike does. Plus it shifted the weight off of the bum, good for rear-end longevity and avoiding any further down-below disasters.

*outlawed by the UCI cycling federation. Any professional cyclist caught puppy-paws'ing can be sentenced to up to 3 years in a French prison.

Utilising the supertuck*, another illegal move, I also got the bike up to a whopping 28mph downhill. That was before I rapidly came to my senses and decided I did not want to arrive in Berlin via ambulance. On a future bike-trip I did take her above 40mph, but it felt dodgy going too fast at this early stage, as the European cobbles had once again shown my sloppy setup. The handlebar bolt had kept loosening, causing the handlebars to twist under pressure. This is not ideal. Most cyclists prefer their handlebars to stay in place and not spin around. Eventually I uber-tightened the bolt late on day 3, to the point of nearly snapping, and it seemed to hold. It was also around this time the back brake randomly stopped working. No idea why. It just suddenly seemed further from the rim. I bodged it with more spacers. This worked □

*Supertuck: Shifting your bum forwards off the seat, so that you are either hovering just above or sitting on the top-tube.

Having already lost a lot of time with one mechanical mishap, the 6 day deadline felt very fragile. If another part of the bike imploded, that could cost another day and make the timing virtually impossible. And we were behind schedule already. So for this reason I'd said I would hotel it until I was back on track and confident of making it. Definitely just for timing and logistical reasons. Nothing to do with me being an absolutely atrocious camper, and getting miniscule, broken sleep.

If you're going for a chilled cycle-touring holiday, then camping is a great money-saving strategy. As previously mentioned, the European campsites are dirt-cheap, with great facilities. But if you're planning on smashing it, then camping becomes a liability. The setting up of the tent is pretty fast. But packing up is painfully time-consuming for me, maybe it's my own disorganisation, or maybe everyone gets this; half my stuff ends up strewn around the tent and needing re-organising and repacking. Then, as demonstrated with the first night, campsite receptions close early. Especially when there's still a lot of summer daylight cycling hours left to be had, You can usually still stay, but it creates complications. You can wild-camp...well legally you can't. But you can break the law. However on paper there are hefty fines in many European countries, and it can differ from state to state even inside Germany. Unless you're a nob I doubt these are ever really enforced, but I don't feel comfortable taking the risk and finding out.

Then when you're setup, if you've been drilling it the whole day, trying to clothe, de-clothe, or just get up for a piss in a one-man tent involve body contortions that are highly likely to cause a cramp explosion. The tent and sleeping pad also add a fair amount of weight and space to your setup. And is tent sleeping really that great? I seem to sleep just as well in a bus-shelter as a tent. So in future when I'm trying to go fast, I am just going to bring a sleeping bag and inflatable pillow. If it is dry, I can find somewhere good enough to kip for a few hours. If the weather is shite, then I hotel it. Simple. When you're bike-tripping you have so much flexibility over where to stay, that you have a huge variety of hotels to pick from. You can invariably find a small, non-touristy town, where the hotels are going to be considerably cheaper.

The 6-day goal still feels do-able fully tenting. But I'll just be trading time spent hanging out with my friend in Berlin, for time struggling stuffing sleeping bags and pads into other bags. I'm working on trying to value my time more, and my money less. So to be true to this, I should hotel it.

Germany seemed to immediately switch from sprawling urban-ness, to a beautiful countryside. It was mainly farmland like the northern Belgian I'd been moaning about, but a bit more variety, trees and undulation.

It was a perfect end to the day. Cruising down a gentle hill. Grinning from ear to ear. Had my self-checkin hotel in Lippstadt booked, 150 miles from where I'd started. Great progress. Endorphins from 11 hours in the saddle. Running high on sugar and caffeine. Jamming to tunes* and snapping pics of beautiful sunset. Usually i dont phone and ride as I'm a nervous nelly. But the (perfect) roads became a ghost town (big football match on?). Genuinely don't think my mood can go higher than it was then. One of those perfect moments in time.

*Just got my "liked songs" on shuffle. Some Foals come on. Tubelord. Johnny Foreigner. Classic indie stuff. "*You don't have my number. Do-doo-do-da-do*"

Fully content and relaxed in the hotel room. Typed up my notes about the day so I didn't forget. Planned my route for tomorrow. The plan: smash it again, so set my alarm for 6am to be off early and had a short-ish, but quality sleep. Finally a proper bed! ♥☐

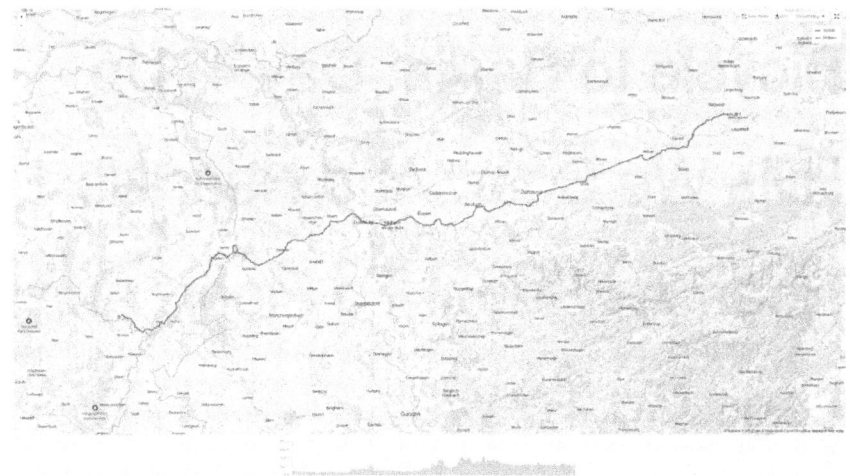

Bicycle to Berlin: Day 4. Up Hills We Soar. And Hear Us Roar. As Pedal To Floor. And Legs Go To War.

I love my special shorts! Its not just that they have pockets. The pockets are on the hips, like cowboy holsters. You feel like Clint Eastwood, quickdrawing sandwiches and flapjacks...Do you feel hungry punk? Why as a matter of fact, yes! Yes I do!

They're a genuine game-changer for long-distance cycling. Even on one-off daily long distance cycles, food in your jersey pockets is such a pain.

- A) You have to contort your arm in awkward ways, which can be cramp-inducing when deep into a big ride.
- B) I've lost countless gloves due to pocketing them when my hands get sweaty, but then accidentally dislodging them later when I pull out a bar from the same pocket.

The special-short pockets are also perfectly placed for surreptitiously pocketing as much of the breakfast buffet as possible. Made off with quite a haul this morning 😋. Hotel breakfasts can often feel a bit pricey to a regular human. But when you are a cycling machine, burning several thousand calories a day, then a continental breakfast for 15 euros becomes a bargain. Literally an infinite supply of high-carb cereal and bread, then so many other pocket-able goodies for the road. Another solid reason to ditch the tent.

So I can push my legs to the limit. But it seems I cannot push Halford essentials zippers to the limit. I have pushed the dangerously over-stuffed pannier-bag a little too far. Zip is borked. Happy with my bodge though. Glad I brought spare straps, and it looks like straps plus duct-tape will hold the clothes bag in.

When I set off, I'm feeling 100 again. This doesn't make logical sense. I smashed 150 miles only several hours before. My body shouldn't have recovered. This seems to be "*The Stage Race Effect*" that professionals describe. Science says your body needs recovery. Science says you'll struggle the next day and must take it easy. But the human body is a magnificent contraption. It adapts like nothing else. The body gets the signal: "*Okay, you've smashed it 3 days in a row. I see where this is going. We're smashing it again. We understand now. Our prime directive is 'make legs go round'. Anything unrelated to the prime directive will be sidelined*". Then it is only after you take a day off, and fully rest… Then everything hits you all at once; your body just capitulates. This is why for grand-tour riders, even on rest days they need to do a multi-hour ride; to avoid this bodily crash. It's either the stage-race-effect, or just the wind changing direction. The good old "*Why am I going so fast? Wind? Nah! Must be my legs are super-strong!*". I could look at the post-ride data and check. But I'd rather be an ostrich and live head-in-sand in my fantasy world, where I have morphed into an unstoppable juggernaut.

And I'm gonna need to be a juggernaut for the day ahead. The area of Germany I battle through is beautiful. Brutal, but beautiful. The central part of Germany is basically a budget Alps. It would be so much fun on a road bike. No mountains, but towering hills, with dense forests and flowing rivers. It makes for pretty special views. Also the hills give you the beauty of altitude, without the

"AAAAAHHH. IM GONNA DIE" feel of descending full-on mountains. I pass through no cities, just quaint villages that resemble their alpine equivalents.

But the views come at a cost. You've got to drag a 25kg bike to the top of them.

Figuratively all of the hills on this trip were condensed into today. Literally about 85% of them. At the top of the first hill, which was several hundred feet alone..... the cycle computer said: "*climb 1/18 completed*". Oh. Oh my.

Going up was hard. Coming down was even harder. I didn't think to bring any spare brake pads. So these need to be conserved for the whole trip. I was using my body to slow us (the bike and I) as much as possible. Doing the "make yourself big" pose that scares away bears (Is it bears? Or badgers? If you do get torn to shreds by a bear, pls dont sue me ☐), or the pose you see motorbike racers doing approaching corners.

Some of the descents are so long my ears are popping. Really is some special scenery. Very few cyclists, but lots of motorbike tourists around. I slightly envy them up the hills.

At the top of the toughest hill of the day I see a sign for the German village of Grossberg. If you know German, you will know this is the most accurately named German village xD

Made the mistake of going gloveless today. My hands aren't too raw. But the sweat from the hills has been pouring into the gear-shifter. It takes so much energy to move it one click round, it's easier to just leave it in 5 and grind out the hills.

Later on in the day the struggle intensifies. I've eaten lots, but it's still not enough. I'm semi-bonking*. Being extremely fat-adapted, I never seem to truly full-bonk. What's fat-adapted? Your body does not simply just burn carbs until it runs out, then switches to fats (and proteins). It is much more complex. Fat-adapted people's bodies will naturally try to use a larger proportion of fat as a fuel source, over carbs. Meaning they should still have more glycogen and carbs available later into an endurance race. The downside being when you want to sprint, or go full-throttle, it's better if your body is carb-adapted, as carbs can be turned into energy "better". They are both faster to metabolise and use up less oxygen for each unit of energy....so if you're out of breath, you want all your oxygen powering carb metabolism.

* For non-cyclists, bonking == hitting the wall in running. Your body has run out of glycogen to convert to sugars, so your blood sugar drops very low, causing you to lose all energy...and then your mind!

Why am I fat-adapted? It may be genetic, or it may be from that time I tried to prove Gandhi was a pussy by fasting for 4 and a half days. Or maybe I just lean into the bonk. I believe when many people's minds start going into dark and weird new places, they recoil from it. They crave retreating to their comfort zone. But it quite intrigues me. It's exciting to let your mind wander new ground. Some people can literally start hallucinating when bonking. I don't think I've visually hallucinated from it. I've seen colours and contrast "pop", similar to the effect of mushrooms. And sometimes it feels like my body is really close to the ground and I'm sinking, like riding a chopper. But it's never worrying. Usually just feels weird. I start playing with my mouth, seeing what weird sounds and demonic voices it can make. BLEURGH! BLARGH! AIIIEIEIEIRRR! People going past probably think I'm Welsh. When I'm not making ridiculous sounds my mouth droops open like a lobotomy victim. It's reached that stage, where the energy expended to keep your lower lip raised and your mouth relatively closed, that energy is gone. It lolls like a blue whale sweeping up krill.

The sugar deficiency gets worse though. Starting the final big climb of the day my legs were at their weakest. I'm going nowhere slowly. Veering over the road like a drunkard coming home at 3am. Then "Satisfied" by "Catching Flies" comes on on my bonephones. My last sugar tablets are kicking in. I stopped trying to pedal. I started dancing. I was flying up the hill. The harder I danced, the faster I flew. Hard to put into words, felt very spiritual.

I finally reach the town of Helmstedt, 157miles from where I started. Done close to 3000metres of climbing (yes I'm mixing metric and imperial). I plop down in an Aldi car park shattered. Shattered, but incredibly proud of myself and the bike. I really want some pizza from the bakery section, but there's a few flies buzzing around it, and thinking it must have been sitting there all day puts me off. Instead I get a tub of vegetarian cevapii (romanian mini-sausauges? No idea why they're here in the middle of Germany), a mega tube of pringles, a falafel wrap, milkshake and finally a coke-zero. I sit in the parking lot, just on the floor with my back up against a wall, munching away as I pick my hotel on my phone. I go for the cheapest one with the cheapest breakfast xD

Another nice hotel, but it's late so I just shower, write up the day and sleep. Oh, I also check comments about my mini write-up of the day before. Gary got a kick out of the "I sat on a bee" sentence. I know it doesn't add any supporting evidence to the "like" vs "like-like" battle, but it still gives me a warm feeling.

Here's what I ate today:
(**editor note**: Probably should have written this down at the time)
Errr...can't remember. A flipping lot. Many thousands of calories. I've been trying to reduce plastic use, but it's hard to make your own flapjacks or snacks on a big trip. So rather than buy little things in lots of small single-use plastic packets, I'd bought a massive loaf of honey-cake. And just

casually took chomps out of a full-sized cake whilst waiting at junctions. Pretty sure this was the day I discovered Beinenstich's from the German bakeries. Also loaded up on doughnuts and croissanty-style things. I still did buy plasticy-wrapped chocolate bars, couple of kitkat chunkies I think. Some flavours I'd never tried before. Oh and I had food I'd snuck into my pockets from breakfast. A big pack of fruit and nuts. Probably way more I've forgotten. Oh yeah, I got through a couple of packets of dextrose tablets, basically raw sugar. I never see them in shops in England.

We've done so well today and yesterday that barring a major catastrophe, we should be storming the Reichstag tomorrow evening. A big, bike breakage buffer has been built up.

Although my powerbank has given up the goat. If my gps machine dies and I have to navigate by hand, I'm more likely to end up in Borneo than Berlin.

I fall asleep well-chuffed. After the first couple of days it had felt like I'd lost my cycling mojo a bit. But the day before I'd raised the bar with 150 miles. And today I'd put it through the fucking roof with 150 miles through hilly Germany.

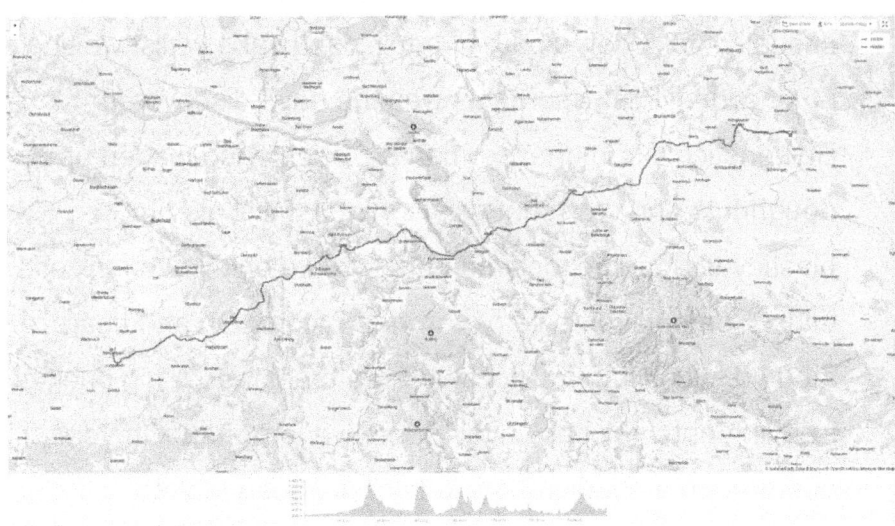

Bicycle to Berlin: Day 5. And So I Arrive. I Have Survive. Bike Still Alive.

Feeling yesterday this time. Legs still flirting outrageously with cramp at breakfast. But I've only got 115 miles left to do. It's in the bag mate!

The sensible option would be to split into two 60 mile days. But it doesn't work like that. Cycling is like music at a party. Once you turn it up to 11, you can't just turn it back down to 10 you square. Feck the neighbours! The intensity dial only goes in one direction! So we're banging this one out today.

I'll be doing this final leg in slippers. Well, sort of slippers. I believe they're surf shoes. I just brought them as a lightweight and foldable pair of "evening" shoes. So far I've been riding with a pair of Adidas five-tens. Can't remember the exact make, the one with the most recycled content iirc from the website. They're specifically designed for cycling on flat-pedal bikes. But it seems like they were designed for short tear-ups around the woods on mountain bikes. Not all-day ultra riding. To maximise power transfer from leg to foot to pedal they're super stiff…but the force goes both ways. Most noticeably in the toe area. My big toes are still slightly numb and definitely sore in the mornings. They've turned purple and I'm concerned the nail might just fall off. So surfing slippers it'll have to be to close out the journey!

Another five-ten annoyance. On flat pedal bikes I like to move my feet around a bit, changing what muscles are bearing the load. Plus it subtly shifts my bum around, preventing any one area from getting too sore. But these shoes are actually too effective at gripping the pedals, it genuinely feels like they're glued on. So when I try to reposition my feet, they often get stuck, and I have to use up mental energy safely picking my feet up to shift them.

After an hour my legs are opening up. Hair of the dog and all that. The dancing revelation makes hills a breeze. I can violently whip the bike from side-to-side, really using its weight against it. I'm whipping it like Matthieu van der Poel whipping anyone who disturbs his slumber*. I'm pounding it on the flats too. The bike has become an extension of my body and mind. There is a deep connection and understanding between us. Having so much fun!

*Hey, this is a cycling book. So I'm allowed to put niche cycling jokes in okay!

I broke my momentum to take a picture of a red squirrel. The whole scenario annoyed me. If I had zero concern of documenting things and proving they happened (to who?

To friends? To future me?), this would have been a nice, short special encounter in nature. It would have left me feeling good and happy to have seen a cool thing. Instead I felt panic as I fumbled with the camera app. The squirrel ran away before I could snap it. So I'd taken an enjoyable moment, and ruined it. I told myself from then on to cool it with the pictures, although I might be being overdramatic. Maybe it's sensible to get the camera out for static things….but just enjoy the moment, when the moment can scuttle away up into the trees!

It is far flatter than the day before, and the scenery more bland. Still some nice woods. But day 4 will be the day to remember. Today is mainly just getting the job done and dusted. It's the first actually sunny day. I'm having to stop far more often to buy extra water, and to reapply sunscreen. I'm very grateful that it stayed cloudy the day before. I can do hills or heat. Both together would have done me in.

I'm on a long road to infinity through the woods for a long stretch. Cannot see where the road ends. It just goes straight. Cars doing 50 mph and fairly busy. So I don't get to enjoy it too much. Spot a hawk of some kind, just 20 feet away from me. Stop to take a photo. It flies away. There's a brief shower during this long forest road, but nothing major.

Further on I turn off onto a cyclepath that runs for miles, roughly following the Elbe river. It's on this stretch that one of my bodges finally fails. My bag of clothes squeezes out of the strapped and duct-taped broken-zipped pannier and thuds onto the tarmac behind me. Best place for it to happen. No cars to run over my clothes. I just double-down on the bodging and use up a third of a roll of duct tape ensuring it won't pop out again.

I'm caressing the bike at this stage. Taking it easy over any bumps. So close. Just don't fall apart. When San jolts I feel pain. I wince as we have to ride over a small, lumpy cobbled sector. San rattling timidly. C'mon, you can make it!

As I pass through Brandenburg, Berlin is almost within touching distance. I no longer feel like parting ways with the bike. Leaving it behind in Berlin would be akin to leaving your dog, or your least favourite child. But the fiends at Eurostar! They won't allow me to rebook the journey from Rotterdam (where bikes aren't allowed), to Brussels (where bikes are allowed) [**editor note**: As of time of writing]. I'd have to fully cancel the ticket, throwing 35€ in the bin, not including the extra 30€ bike ticket on the new one.

Some people say you can't put a price on love.
Not me. My price is a firm 50€. You've got to draw the line somewhere. And love won't pay off a mortgage.
People also say:

> *If you love someone, set them free. Or push them into a canal. And if they love you, they'll find their way back to you.*

So I'm going to stand firm. The bike has got to go. And being a penny-pincher, I've decided that after reaching the goal, I don't need to splooge on expensive Berlin hotels. If I dragged this 2kg tent halfway across Europe; we might as well get some bloody use out of it. This decision will lead to regret :)

Whilst pausing for a drink and food break, I decide on a campsite on the Western side of Berlin, 11 miles from the centre. This means I can rapidly check-in and pay before reception closes, and then cycle back late after reaching the centre. Smart? That was the plan anyway. This strategic blunder turns the finale of the trip into a bit of a failed orgasm. The smart plan would have been to call it quits for the day. Despite being tantalising close and within touching distance of the goal. I could have a proper meal at the fancy campsite restaurant. I'd wake up early and eager. Raring to go. Triumphantly rolling into Berlin and the Brandenburg gate. Revelling in the experience. Enjoying a sumptuous victory breakfast. But exhaustion make brain go slow. Me no think too well.

I still regret missing the breakfast finish opportunity to this day. Instead my tunnel-vision "*derrr...Gotta get to central Berlin*" brain decided it **must** finish the adventure that night. The campsite checkin has me boiling with frustration. Cycling 420 miles in 3 days leaves you a tad tetchy and impatient: "*Yeah it's nice you're having a lovely conversation with the receptionist. But maybe you can see there are multiple other people behind you. With shit to do. Places to be. Charity cycles to finish. So....y'know?*"

Then when it came time for me to book in. Dear God. After giving my passport to the young, braided receptionist: "*Clack.................Clack..............Clack...........Clack*". I wince at each painfully slow keystroke. People say "*oh, you shouldn't keep your emotions bottled up. You should release them into the world*". But what the fudge are you supposed to do in this situation? "*Hi, have you considered typing slightly faster than my Grandma? Have you considered not being completely inept at what is surely 60% of your job?*". There's nothing you can say without being a nob. So there's nowhere for the anger to dissipate. It just burrows down deep inside you. My mind is melting from frustration.

So I'm leaving the campsite already seething. Trying to mentally wrestle my emotions back into a good and nice place. I should be over the moon. I'm about to have done the thing! I wanted to do the thing! I'm proud I done the thing!....but the fatigue overwhelms me and I cannot grasp onto these thoughts. I just sink into the sulk.

Now everything irritates me. My sunglasses are smeared with suncream and greasy food. It's getting dark and I can barely see my cycle-computer through them. Plus it would also be freeing to take the glasses off. Enjoy the sights as they should be seen, with your real eyes…Aaaaand the moment I take them off; my eyes are bombarded by flies. Fuckers! I'm blinking and clawing at my eyes to fish one out. Fuck! This! Sunglasses back on. So I'm straining my now stinging eyes to see the route and turns. What else can I find to complain about? The cyclepaths? The cyclepaths in outer Berlin are shite. They're glorified pavements, jolting and bolting me and the bike all over the shop.

What the fuck am I doing? Dragging myself reluctantly into Berlin. Down a long hill, which I'm only gonna have to climb back up an hour later. Why? What for? My mind is turning on itself. "*Are you doing this just so you can tell people you cycled to Berlin in 4.5 days rather than 5? Do you think they fucking care? Is your ego so fragile you're prepared to ruin the climax like this*". I also really need a poo.

Through the suburbs and into the Charlottenburg part of Berlin. I haven't really gone through the main part of a big city on this trip. Dortmund is certainly a big city, but the cyclepath didn't go through the trendy parts. Although lets be honest, does Dortmund have trendy parts? I see couples strolling around hand-in-hand, enjoying the calm summer evening. Fashionably dressed people, with bags from designer clothing stores. A feeling of supreme disconnection washes over me. I seem so so far away from these people. My clothes stagnant. Back erupting in sweaty backpack spots. Skin a congealed mess of cream and sweat. Hair matted and straggly. Not just physically we're disconnected. They're probably off to a nice restaurant, excitedly chattering about their day. Their life. I can't step into a nice restaurant in this filthy state. Instead I dive into a minimart, buy a pack of biscuits and a 3-part desert contraption. I squat on a street corner, wolf it down like some kind of yoghurt goblin. This is not a befitting way to celebrate a great accomplishment. Then they'll be going home, maybe after a fancy cocktail or two, to their snug bed. Whilst I limp back to my tiny tent, cowering from the mosquitoes, afraid to go brush my teeth. Sigh.

When I get to Tiergarten, a big park with the Brandenburg gate at one end, my mood ebbs and chills a bit. Cycling through a nice park, tall trees and no cars will do that. The stress of cycling through manic city traffic had probably amplified the negative, disconnected feelings. So at least I'm managing to savour the very final hundreds of metres. Coasting along, mainly thinking back to the epic day 4 with all the hills. I arrive at the Brandenburg Gate, it's swarming with tourists so I hop off and walk. A couple ask a stranger to take their pic with the gate, so I in turn ask the couple for a pic of me and the bike. In the photo I look genuinely delighted. There definitely was a brief moment of happiness. Even if it was not basking in the glow of achievement and contentment like it could have been the following morning. Although I'm not sure why I need to slightly crouch down in every photo of me, as if standing tall means the photographer won't be able to get me and the Brandenburg gate in frame. How tall do I think I am?

The elation didn't last long. It was replaced by...nothing really. Just calm. But that's OK. Like when you've had a work week 3x more stressful than usual. And it's finally over. And you instinctively take a big, deep breath. Your first deep breath all week (note: I should start doing daily deep breathing stuff. Maybe you should too?). I let the calm envelop me and set off backtracking to the tent. Tomorrow I'll text my friend to meet up, head into Berlin, and figure out how to have a "proper" holiday for the 2 days I still have left here.

Bicycle to Berlin: Change of Plans

Epic cycling bit is over, so I'm not gonna bore you with too many details of the regular holiday part:

- I Hung out with my friend
- Jeff was alright
- Ditched the bike
- Went to Rotterdam
- Ate the mushrooms
- Asked Gary if she wanted to go out sometime. She said yes! Over the moon? More like over the sun!

.......Aaaaand everything above was a lie! Well except hanging out with my friend. That was cool and chill. We got the best ice-cream I've ever eaten. Hokey-pokey. Also the salad bar at bistro Lebenswelten on Museum Island was amazing, and they mistakenly undercharged us by 50%. Score. I'm noting a strong obsession with food here. Blaming the calorie deficit from the trip. Oh, whilst I'm here, move over Belgian Bakeries. The Germans are the new King. Neu Kungen. So many great things to choose from.

Genuinely too many tasty unique bakery goods for me to pick a standout. I love them all equally. They all belong inside my belly. Plus I've completely forgotten all their names because they were in German. Pretty sure I'm going to end this several hundred mile trip having increased in mass. Oh, a non-food highlight was cycling around the abandoned airfield in the middle of Berlin. Pretty epic.

But onto the ruses:

Jeff was fucking amazing. Double encore. Electric energy. Gary said "I've already got plans for friday"...oh well :/

Wasn't distraught, just deflated. Like your football team that's been stuck in mid-table League One for 12 years conceding a last minute winner in the play-off finals. It was nice to dream of a better life in the championship, but we're used to League One, we're content there. The grounds are usually a bit more charming and the hotdogs are cheaper. We'll search for a new striker and then maybe next year is our year anyway.

.

What else was a lie? Oh the Rotterdam plan has well and truly gone out the fucking window. There's that. No mushrooms for me. Although it didn't really feel like I needed them. The trip itself has been transformational enough.

I could not bring myself to abandon the bike. Well I could, but I'd been a bit naive on European train prices: "*Oh European trains are always so cheap compared to Britain. No need to pre-book anything*". Well well well; sitting in a cafe, enjoying a final baked good and sipping my coffee, I'm about to head to the station and go to double-check the train timings…u wot? My 40 euro train has suddenly become 140 euro? Err…no thanks. When researching travel methods I had noticed an overnight sleeper train from Berlin, which went direct to Rotterdam and did simple bike tickets you could select as you checked out. But it seemed a bit expensive back then. The sleeper train from Berlin → Rotterdam is still only 79 euros, with an extra 20 for the bike. So doing the maths, it would now be cheaper to take the bike back on the overnight train than get a regular train. It's Tuesday afternoon right now. I'm back to work at 9am on Thursday. The overnight train will get me to Rotterdam Wednesday morning. Could I ride all the way from Rotterdam → Dunkerque and get a Wednesday overnight ferry? Crazier things have happened. e.g. Women's menstrual cycles. Imagine your genitals being controlled by the moon. What in the fuck. The weather forecast is not good. Dry, but a block headwind all the way down the coast. I've done the Dutch coast in headwinds before. It's not pretty. On one of the windiest days of the year they literally host headwind riding championships in Bad-Cadzand, precisely where I'll be riding through. If we try this, it's gonna get a bit gruesome. But we've come this far?

I'm still sleep deprived and not quite with it, I feel a bit like a passive observer as I see myself rescheduling my Eurostar, cancelling the Rotterdam hostel, booking the sleeper. But if Mr Lizard thinks we can do it, then it's on! :D

My sleep deprived brain may just have been using this as an excuse to cancel the Rotterdam hostel. I really want to love tents and hostels. It would be so convenient for my bank balance, also the social aspect...but mainly the bank balance. But just no. No. Let's rewind to how I ended up with almost no sleep in Berlin:

Camping: First nights in Berlin I camped outside the city as you remember. I carefully selected a spot for my tent based on angles and gradients and proximity to the toilets to avoid tripping over other tents in the middle of the night. The spot had no grass underneath but should that matter? Both nights I failed to sleep. The ground was rock solid. Blimey, I have never truly appreciated grass.

When I packed up the tent....my sleeping pad would not deflate. Am I using the valve wrong? Is it broken?.....Oh. I'd accidentally sat on the valve and 90% deflated it upon pitching.

So I'd been trying to sleep on literally nothing, just the hard ground. But had also been kept awake by the itching. The first night I had made the grievous mistake of trying to enjoy the evening outside my tent. This led to an initial feeding frenzy, after which I had the bug net closed at all times. But

I'm still getting bitten. How? Where? I could not understand. Is there one trapped in here with me?

Whilst tearing down the tent, I discovered the corpses of two squashed red ants and a medium sized spider. I don't think they appreciated being squashed, and demonstrated their displeasure with their fangs.

The camping was intense....... (I think this joke is a lot cleverer than it is funny, but I am very proud of it so I'm leaving it in xD). By my reckoning, a (good) hostel on gig night would have been an upgrade. Nope. They gave me a top bunk. There was no ladder. "Excuse me, how do I get up there?" I asked one of my roommates.

"*You have to just vault it. Like a gymnast*"

Great. I am not a gymnast. Woke everyone else in the room up with my clumsiness. Then realised the top bunk was a paltry 3 feet wide....with no railing.

In the past I've been told I can be a very "dynamic" sleeper. Like a dog actively dreaming. I dream kung fu. Not feeling keen to faceplant the floor on my final night, I barely slept. So hopefully, really hopefully, hope-against-hopefully…the sleeper train will be better? I really need a night of good sleep.

I'm regretting taking the bike for a treat on what should have been its "last day". We went for a spin off-road in the woods. Berlin has lots of woods on its outskirts. I saw several mountain bikers starting or finishing their rides as I trekked back and forth between camp and centre. We started on lovely roads. But when some nice forest paths beckoned us, why not? Why not? Because the sand-filled chain now makes angry grinding noises. I give it an attempted GT-85 and rag clean in a park. The most memorable part of the wood excursion was the fox I shared breakfast with. Cashews and cranberries. I hope foxes can eat those OK. This one looked very sad. It was so tame, pretty sure it was quite ill. It looked incredibly tatty, fur missing, raggedy bony ribs. It chomped away like it was the first meal it'd had in a while. I was the one having to keep the distance. Mainly due to a phobia of dying from rabies. Is it a phobia if you should genuinely be scared of it?

The sleeper train was actually alright. Yeah! Bottom bunk baby! Could only really sleep until 5:30 am, as people in my room were getting off earlier in Amsterdam. But still better than the hostel or tents.

I was getting nervous about the big ride from Rotterdam. I noticed on the train announcements the next station after Rotterdam would be Antwerp, I hadn't realised that. Antwerp would cut at least 30 miles off the trip, and avoid the Vlissingen to Breskens ferry crossing as you hop across the final chain of 3 big Dutch islands on the coast. This is going to be really do-able now, I'm fired up!

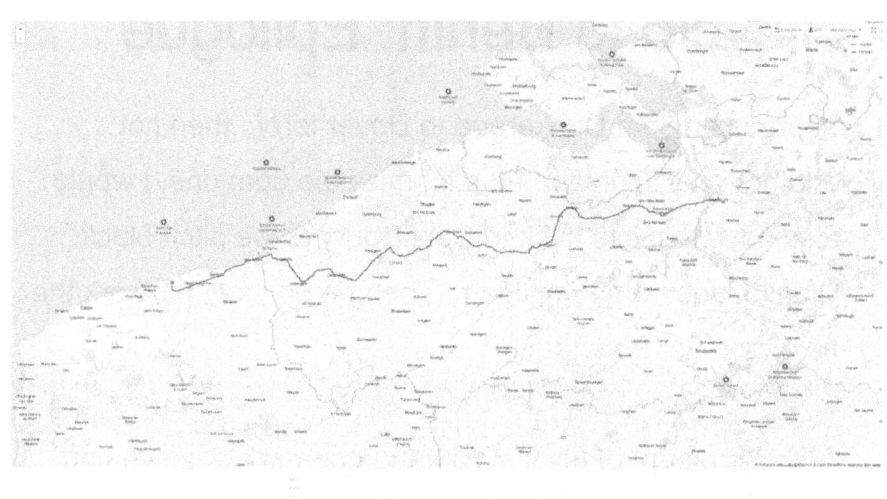

115

Bicycle to Berlin: Epilogue

There is an 8pm Dunkerque to Dover ferry...then not another until midnight! Plus if I miss the 8pm one, I would also have to cycle back to Canterbury in the pitch black. Wouldn't be home until 3am. Then be up early for work the next day. Far from ideal.

At this moment of my life, with the poorest sleep I've had since...ever?....all I want in the world is to be snuggled up in my perfect, comfy bed. But making the 8pm ferry would require an average speed of 14 mph. That is 14 mph factoring IN every stop and junction. So more like 16mph when actually riding. There's the concern that attempting the 8pm ferry job would turn the day into misery, a world of pain...possibly to still miss it by minutes anyway. But as they say: Better to never try at all, than to try and fail anyway!!! I would go at a pace I wanted to, and see how the day transpired.

A panicked start. Prepping myself for the cycle I'm sniffing some Olbas oil as we are pulling into Antwerp. I use Olbas to open up the airways, feels like I can push harder if my nose isn't stuffy. Damn I must have sniffed a bit too hard. Suddenly blood is streaming out of my nose. I barely get the nosebleed under control by the time we fully stop. But there's still blood all over my chin. No time to dally though. Leaving the train I couldn't spot any elevators. So I yolo'd the stairs. How many could there be? Turns out Antwerp station has platforms 4 levels deep. □

Saying that trying to run up many stairs with the super heavy bike was hard, is an understatement. I was doing involuntary gym roars. Definitely very macho roars. Not at all pathetic or weird. Weird looks from people travelling the other way. Not everyday you see a man covered in blood, with a massive bike-packing setup covered in flowery stickers, lugging it up the stairs whilst roaring. But I'm a man on a mission and every second might count.

Then I haemorrhage another 15 minutes outside the station. All mapping software seems to be suggesting I swim across a massive river. No thanks. Ride around in circles frantically searching for a way across, the nearest bridge being aeons away. Eventually I discover the subterranean entrance to the cycling river portal. A bland non-descript, squat building from the road-side, on the other side it houses a big set of steel elevator doors. It takes us down to a long tunnel that goes all the way under the river and out the other side.

Once I am "going"..."going" is an over-exaggeration. Figuratively falling asleep on the bike. My legs have been chilling in Berlin, but the days of shitty sleep are really catching up to me. It's not that my legs burn and can't be pushed more. It's just all-over-body tiredness.

My kickstand has wobbled loose, and it needs an 8mm allen key to tighten it. My multi-tool only goes up to 6mm. At first it just made a rattling sound, making the bike even more vocal than usual. But it has become so loose that it was starting to swing wildly about, and in danger of getting caught in the pedals, which I don't know the outcome of. But it probably ends up with me and the bike on the ground.

So after only a couple hours of riding, I have to stop and duct-tape the stand to the frame. I'd also managed to snap a strap on my sleeping bag and have to duct tape that as well. God bless duct tape.....but so far I had averaged 12.3 mph...the dream seems dead. This is so far short of the 14mph average that only a monster could pull it back in the 2nd half. It would be insane to make the 8pm ferry.

I'd basically given up, and was planning to just have a leisurely late-lunch in Diksmuide (a nice town with nice cafes). But after I'd absolutely cleared out the croissant section of a local bakery things picked up. I was suddenly going faster and faster. No pain or struggle, feeling good. 15 mph. 16. 17. 18 mph at times..... and my legs weren't burning at all. My heart-rate was high and I was breathing hard, but it felt good. I was really getting into the zone and revelling in seeing the average speed tick up and up. Just a 0.1 mph here and there. But my body and the bike were flying.

As I reached the outskirts of Diksmuide, it was suddenly seeming possible..... but still only achievable if I absolutely buried myself. If I had no leisurely lunch, then 16/17 mph all the way until Dunkerque port, that could pull it off. Minor stomach cramps told me I was already close to the limit.

Prioritisation of blood to muscles over the digestive system. But fuck it, let's give it a crack!

As we flew through Diksmuide without stopping, I guzzled the remaining pastries and pressed even harder on the pedals. No pain au chocolat. No gain au chocolat! I sunk my forearms on handlebars, bum out, doing the best Remco impersonation I could, my mind started playing the guitar solo from "The Chain". Dun.....du-du-dun...du-du-da-da-da-dun-dun.....C'mon!

As you get close to the coast, the wind gets stronger, the headwind kicked up. Hammering it. Watching the clock tick towards the deadline. Pretty dehydrated. Focused on pedalling. Nothing stops the rhythm. I did not think I could push that hard for multiple hours. The power of a comfy bed!

I pulled up to the check-in gate 5 mins after checkin officially closed....

"Am I...in...time...for the.....the 8pm?"

A young, Japanese-ish looking face, with a warm smile: sure, that's fine. just need your ticket and passport

Waves of relief. Emotionally this was bigger than reaching Berlin :smile:

I'm in bed with the bike by 11pm. First good nights sleep in sooo long

Interlude: A typical day in the life of an Extremely Senior Rearend Engineer at Generic Finance Company

So to break up the rides I'm putting in some "day in the life" of stuff, showcasing my usual mundane life, in contrast to the wacky cycling adventures. Work asked me to write a piece for their website….and then regretted it after seeing how weird I'd made it. The antithesis of LinkedIn. But at least I can put it in here, so wahey.

(**note to editor**: I expect some of the nerdy computery terms to go over peoples heads. But I feel like leaving them in gives more of a flavour of my usual day. How it can feel a bit abstract and disconnected from reality at times [even if it's still fun!]. Definitely not just because I'm too lazy to rewrite it). Here we go:

Twetwe...twe...chir...chip..twe..twee...twoo. No, I've not had a stroke. I am waking to the soothing sounds of synthetic birds. Tropical birds. No, I'm not in the Amazon rainforest. I'm in Canterbury. In a crumbling Victorian terraced house; built years before I was even a twinkle in the eyes of people I have only seen in photographs. A house described by the estate agent as "cosy" and "full of charm". Why do estate agents find damp so charming? Why does the profession attract such ardent mycophiles? The sound comes from the radio-alarm, tropical birds to differentiate from the British words outside the windows. 10 seconds in a Toucan blares: "*YARGAGAAGAHH*!!" It's mixed 5x louder than the rest. I fly out of bed, leaping across the room. Silence it before it can wake the whole damn neighbourhood.

Pop downstairs and brew myself a Lemsip. Oooh...that's the good stuff. Got over the cold weeks ago; still smashing the stuff. You can see why they use it to make crystal meth. Start work around 9 as the 'sip starts to hit. Laptop on. I3 tiling window manager on Linux :Finger Guns:. Stable Ubuntu :the opposite of finger guns:. No more Arch Linux for me. Too old for living on the bleeding edge. Slack, Firefox and Pycharm open. Respond to any early slack messages. Vote on whether we do the non-daily daily standup. No-one votes yes, nice! 8)

Setup: Single monitor nowadays, minimises distractions. But I've got a proper desk; with legs and everything. I can't be leaving a hot laptop on my crotch all day.... I'm trying for a baby. With whom you ask? I'm actually not fussed whom. Any womb will do. Whom's womb? Any!

The main point is that I get some heirs out there. Pronto. I need them running around and capable of wielding swords, before civilization collapses. If not swords, then at least bits of 2x4 with kitchen knives taped to them. Watching recent geopolitical developments, that day of reckoning could be upon us sooner rather than later. Got to be ready. Ready for when I slaughter my way to Chief Warlord of the East Kent area (including but not limited to the Wantsum Marshes Wasteland). I cannot be dealing with conquering, annihilating, *and* raising a family all at the same time. Well not raise them per se, but like, check in at least once a year, make sure they ain't being allowed to watch anime or anything like that. Pokemon's alright, but none of that Evangelion shite.

Machiavelli says: *If you kill a ruler, to avoid being revenge-assassinated yourself, you must wipe out his entire family.* Or something along those lines. I'm parrot-phrasing. So I'm thinking maybe around 23 or so little-ones should render it sufficiently impractical for any would-be assassin, at least from an administrative perspective. 23 is probably overkill, but it's better to be on the safe side.

I open up Gitlab to crack some code reviews first. We work right to left. Nothing more annoying than being responsible for a project, which people are waiting on. And then it's just stuck, sat there, waiting for review, like a turd that won't flush. Well actually there's lots of things more annoying. Getting a piece of food stuck in your teeth, which is impossible to dislodge via tongue. Why aren't toothpicks more normalised in our society? Do people just walk around putting up with shit between their teeth all day? Madness. I wonder if getting your tongue pierced would enable you to clear debris more effectively? Something to ask my dentist; the next time I chip my tooth on a stale naan, or from forgetting that chickens have bones, or from falling off a campervan. But I digest...the point is, waiting for reviews is annoying.

Reviews smashed (I have a checklist/self-guide for what I need to check. If I don't give myself lists and rules like these I can be a tad slapdash and forget things. TODO: link it here, or put in appendix? Probably can't be fucked. If you go to the appendix and it's not there, then I'm sorry.)

Spoke too soon. Someone's up-thumbed the 11am standup. Sigh. Put on some trousers. Grab my little widget of curiosities; toying with it supposedly helps focus during meetings. Otherwise I just end up covertly reading slack or writing code until it's..."Who me? errr could you repeat the question. I think my connection's slightly unstable".

5 minutes until meeting. Not enough time to do anything. So I go and feed the birds. Today I deliberately avoid putting out Crow-friendly food. Crows are surprisingly intelligent creatures, nearly as intelligent as Django developers. If feeding them every day becomes routine, they can become extremely demanding. Lining up menacingly outside your window at 6am, quacking loud enough to wake up the whole neighbourhood (note: Nope! You're wrong. Ducks Wack. Crows Quack. Use your ears before you use your mouth bellend!*). The final straw was on a bleary morning, when one flew into my open bedroom window. Absolute havoc. After this I gave them a stern talking to. I'll feed them some days, but other days they're to fend for themselves. And no amount of quacking will sway me.

*I've since been reliably informed that I don't actually have Crows, they're Jackdaws. So I guess I am the bellend in this situation, like so many other situations.

The Crows have also agreed to stop eating my dreams. Which was a relief at first, but now the nightmares have returned. In the nightmares my house is overrun by mice. In reality my house is also overrun by mice, but in reality I am too lazy to do anything about it. In my dreams an exterminator, usually called Roger, provides me with a high-tech, still-in-alpha-testing new form of poison. It doesn't just kill the mouse. Oh no. It infects the brain. The mouse begins to crave. It craves the taste of brains, the brains of it's brethren. Eradicating an entrenched rodent population via poison can be a lengthy ordeal lasting weeks. This virus spreads through the mouse population like wildfire. Within days every mouse in the area is dead, or hunting those that aren't. In my dream I am walking downstairs for lunch one-day, when I spot something in the corner of the living room. A healthy mouse: It's back against the wall. Whiskers taut. Beady eyes flicking left and right. Desperately searching for an escape route. It's surrounded by several infected-mice. Patchy fur, chunks of flesh missing. It makes my stomach turn. They edge closer. Should I try and save the mouse? Didn't I want them all gone? Before I can act, the mouse makes a break for it. It barrels towards the widest gap in the encirclement. There's not enough space. Hind quarters wedged between two of the infected. It struggles, my heart rises as it looks like he may break free. No. The infected clamp their teeth into his thighs. Pinned down, the others swarm over him. He's torn to shreds. I'm so engrossed by the horrific scene, I fail to notice a single infected mouse had split off from the group. I feel something crawl over my foot, up my ankle. I panic and shake. But that just makes it sink it's teeth in. Flash of pain. Motherfucker! I flinch, causing it to be thrown slightly upwards. In midair, I absolutely fucking welly it. 'Ave It. It is propelled across the room. Arcs gracefully towards the kitchen window. Hits the top-corner with a meaty thud. (I adopt the voice of former "The Day Today" sports journalist and all round great guy Sir Alan Partridge) "Ster-riiiiker! Now THAT, was liquid football."

Barring the self-satisfaction of still having got it, footballing-wise….the whole experience has left me feel slightly nauseous. I go and have a little lie down. I'm getting a headache. Fever?

Wake the next day, grogged as fucked, but with an insatiable hunger. The insatiable hunger is for mice brains. For fucks sake. This is really going to hinder my social life.

And it does. My friends and family become "concerned" about me. The main bone of contention is my newfound habit: Mid convo, pulling out a pocket-mouse and chomping it's head clean off. My behaviour has become "uncouth" and "disturbing".

Then mid disastrous dinner-date, I usually wake (for real*) in cold-sweat.

*This reality. The one you're reading this in.

It's your usual tech-standup. How are people getting on? Any blockers? Who's done the biggest poo this morning? Quick questions. Etc.

Meeting over. I jump into pycharm, coding whatever needs doing. I work in the finance team. So it's a mix of integrating with payment/banking providers, automating compliance checks, writing admin tools for our operations team, or ledgering to track where all the money is.

Hmmm....money you say? Have I thought about doing an office space? Of course I have. Who hasn't? I'm not afraid of prison: 3x meals cooked for you a day. Meet a bunch of new friends; can probably even airbnb the house whilst I'm away. Seems like a win-win-win to me. But I enjoy working here, and I imagine siphoning rounding errors into my bank account must be frowned upon. Verbal warning minimum.

Note: I am quite clearly joking. We take processing money stuff accurately seriously. Plus out of every company I've worked with, Generic Finance Company has had the most thorough approach to security. Helps a lot that the CTO has a security background.

This next paragraph is going to sound like disgusting shilling. But I've been here over 2 human years. That's 14 in dog years, or 28 in software dev years. So it is genuine: Payments/finance work sounds trivial and boring on paper. But because Generic Finance Company can cover so much of the buyer flow, there's a much higher level of complexity than you'd think. Which makes the work engaging and challenging for me. But at the end of the day, if I write a bug, nobody dies (so far). So working with money is the perfect balance of tension vs sleeping soundly.

So yeah. Write some code. Write some tests. Stop for lunch. Write some docs or decision records....less than I really should, but better than nothing. Like single-ply toilet roll (tangent: genuinely the worst thing about the London office is the toilet paper. When we first moved there I was pilfering a couple of rolls each time I came in. But I'm so fed up with it, the tables have reversed. Now I bring my own triple-quilted supply into the office. Don't worry; I'm absolutely rinsing them on the milk instead.).

Similar to earlier, right-to-left, I focus on touching up in-review tickets before starting new stuff. Can I elaborate? Maybe? I don't like test driven development so I don't do it*. Pycharm debugger is my rock. My Automat Kalashnikov. Who writes print statements in 2024? Losers, that's who. To me, "Good code" is trying not to think too hard. Maybe because I'm a man of science, but what's wrong with just using functions**? ¯_(ツ)_/¯. Half of my time is spent naming and working out where to put code. Writing that out feels a bit eek, as that's a very AI replaceable part; although the positive way to spin it is being AI "off-loadable"; thus giving me double the time to clarify specs and argue with product managers. Yay :| ***

*(Sometimes when writing code, it unearths unexpected trinkets, which change feature specs, force concessions, or anything that would invalidate any pre-written tests)

**(I'm over-exaggerating slightly, but I still find that if I start off writing pure functions, then refactor into classes......I end up with something much neater and simpler than trying the reverse. Maybe you can just write things perfectly first-time. Good for you. Cunt.)

***(note: joking. I never seem to spend time pleading to cut down scope here.)

Lunch: Bread. Can't beat good bread. A loaf a day; keeps the mild dread at bay.

Give us this day our daily bread,
or you I'll put in a hospital bed.
I've got a knife. I've got some butter.
Your bread or your life? There's nowhere to scutter.
I've told you once. I've told you twice.
Think of your children. Think of your wife.
Do not dilly. Do not dally.
Or you'll wind up, dead in this alley.
A glint and a slice, there goes your life.

And as you lay dead, I claim that sweet, soft bread.

...

My favourite film is Judge Dredd.

That poem was called "*The Bread Mist Descends*". I hope it conveys the depths of my feelings for bread. Thankyou.

Post lunch

After lunch I put on my headphones to drown out the sorrow (Music: Anything from abrasive noise pop to ambient clunge). Working from home has some great benefits. But you are at the full mercy of your environment, especially your neighbours. 4 months ago mine got a light-brown, half-sausage puppy, which is left alone for multiple hours during the day. It is very cute. It also has very severe attachment issues. Every time it whines, I die a little more inside. Hopefully it is winter when I become fully undead. I yearn to be a frost-lich. To smite my foes with ice magic. The mosquitoes that infest the woods by my house, they will suffer the full extent of my wrath.

"We're hoping he'll grow out of it". Spoiler: He ain't flipping growing out of shit. I really should offer to dogsit. I still haven't. I wonder if that's because a) Whilst I put on appearances of putting others first.....when the cookie crumbles, I'd rather let it suffer, over mildly inconveniencing myself. Do I really want to take in a hyperactive fiend that nibbles half of my furniture, and piddles on the other. Only I'm allowed to piddle on my furniture. b) Or,is it because I tend to overthink every social situation and end up coming across completely unhinged. "There's no need to worry.......I have zero plans of eating him"..... "Well we weren't worried about that at all. But now we are very alarmed. Never talk to me or my dog again."

I close out the day with more of the same really. There's a decent amount of async discussion with product/stakeholders. No obligation to context switch to it, I understand the majority of softies hate context switching. But I enjoy bouncing around different things. Similarly if someone reports a bug with an area under my jurisdiction, I'll usually pounce on it. Raargh! I'm a lion. Bug-fixing is the most fun part of devving. I'm a bit of a flip-flopper, so the new-feature trade-off decisions you're forced to make always brings angst. A bug is usually a bug, and there is a clear and defined fix. You also get to feel like Miss Marple, but with a crazy twist; turns out you were the murderer this whole time!

If it's an easy fix, Shia Lebouf that shit. No need to check if there's enough points in the sprint or waterfall or whatever the fuck the agile kids are sniffing these days. JUST DO EET. And by "JUST DO IT" I mean get a peer to thoroughly review and test the change. Let's not go too mental. We're not Will Smith from Wild Wild West.

I don't like ending the day on a red pipeline or tests. So I'll usually plug away until it's fixed. A green pipeline soothes the soul and I'm away.......... ✓

The End

The day after this I was keen to do some drugs, not mushrooms though. The average ketamine lasts just over an hour, making it the perfect lunchtime drug. So I called up my dealer an hour before lunch break. She turned up on a moped with a big Deliveroo box holding the stuff.

"Don't you know the police are onto dealers dressing up as food delivery people?"

"Yeah, but look in the box. There's an actual McDonalds meal in there. Fools them every time"

"But won't that food be disgustingly cold?"

"Precisely….So realistic."

At this moment the car drove past. The window rolled down. The sun glinting off the black. Time slowed down. The rat-a-tat-tat. The thuds into wood. Into bricks. Into flesh. No screams. But the sound of air being forced out of lungs. I flung the door shut. It didn't shut. A yelp. Fingers in the door frame. The door swings back open. Fingers retreat. Again. This time it slams shut. Scratching at the door. Whimpering. Too quiet to make out the words, like the TV on slightly too loud next door. My Pomodoro timer goes off. Telling me my 1o minute break is over, and it's another 50 minutes of intense concentration and focus before lunch. I find it hard to concentrate with the scratching, so I put on my noise-cancelling headphones and select a bit of thumping techno. It's hard to concentrate during the 50 minutes though. What am I going to have for lunch? Burrito or pasta? I feel like pasta, but I had that yesterday as well. Don't want to get too bored of pasta. Can you get bored of pasta? I go for pasta. Simple pesto pasta with some mushrooms, and some top-drawer sourdough bread to mop up the sauce. What a great lunch. Amazing how a good meal can completely turn your day around.

I probably should have used that day for the day in the life thing. Oh well.

Coast2Coast: Bodged chase the sun

The longest day of each year is in mid June. On the longest Saturday there are official "chase the sun" rides at many places around the world. The idea is you start on the beach, on the East coast at sunrise….and you're racing or chasing the sun. Trying to beat it; make it to the beach on the West Coast before it sets. If you achieve this then you win. The sun loses.

They have an Italian version, a Scottish version, Irish, Northern England and Southern England. And there's probably more dotted around the globe.
All the ones I've listed are roughly 200 miles. They are a major single day challenge, not for newbie cyclists.

The year before I had done the Southern England one...sort of. The official route runs from the Isle of Sheppey to

Weston-super-Mare. I could not be arsed with booking a hotel on Sheppey. So I just started from my house in Canterbury and rode upwards, joining the official route in North Kent.

The attempt last year was the most enjoyable single day ride I've done. Quite a few people living along the route seem to know about it. So they come out of their houses and cheer for you, especially nearer the end. It's a cracking atmosphere. On most sportives (fancy word for a big organised bike-ride), I do feel sorry for the drivers who can inadvertently end up stuck behind 20 different groups of cyclists. On a normal day out, losing a bit of time to cyclists isn't the end of the world. But there are so, so many people on many of these sportives. I would not want to be stuck behind one in a rush. Maybe we shouldn't be rushing about everywhere so much, especially on our relaxing off-days, but whatever. Sometimes you've got to get somewhere by a time, and you haven't accounted for there being 400 cyclists out in your path. So I still feel bad, especially if it's not too much of a challenging sportive, and is more just a nice, chilled day in the sun. However Chase the Sun, being over 200 miles, and spanning coast to coast...feels so much more epic than any other sportive. Such a gruelling challenge, such a test of endurance. So whilst riding it I don't care about holding up drivers. It feels like their inconvenience is worth this grand trial. It also helps that the huge distance splits people up a bit more. You still keep coming across fellow challengers, but you're not swarming the roads with them. And the bike-handling skills and road awareness of people trying these mega events seems higher than usual. If you're consistently doing over 100 mile rides, then if you don't ride ultra sensibly…the law of probability will catch up with you sooner or later. So yeah, so many reason, but I love this ride.

For 2024 I wanted to do it again. But I wanted to make this one tougher than last year. How could I make it tougher? I could try it on my hybrid bike? But I feel uncomfortable when I bomb past people on their much fancier road bikes, like I'm showing off. So that leaves making it longer. Making it slightly longer would also mean I could actually start on the coast, at Ramsgate harbour, thus making it a real coast 2 coast. That sounded like a good plan.

I didn't actually know I was going to do it until 3 days beforehand. In fact I actually missed it on the official date, the longest Saturday of the year. I'd been thinking that my Berlin escapades was enough epic riding for the year. That I should work on revelling in my accomplishments a bit more, rather than: "Done! What's next then?". So the plan had been to chill for the rest of the year, and leave some of my other cycling goals (mainly 250mile ride and everesting) to be earnt next year....but then I couldn't help myself. It had been a while since Berlin, and my body was aching to push itself to the limit. Fuck it. I can do it a weekend late. On my own. Bodged as fuck. But I'll still do it. The plan is:

- Start at home
- Cycle to Ramsgate for sunrise (I don't want to burden family, asking them to give me a lift so early in the morning), it's only about 18 miles, you can bomb it along the main-ish road when there's no cars.
- Then from Ramsgate all the way across to Weston-super-mare for sunset. Totalling 250 miles. It's now noticeably longer than the official route...and I've got a shorter day to do it in...but it feels do-able. I think I'll always be able to push myself to keep going, it's just doing it fast enough to beat sunrise that'll be the tricky bit.

On the Wednesday I booked the hotel for Saturday night meaning I was now committed. On the Thursday I was going into the London office for drinks. I used it as an opportunity to get in some last minute training and miles, so cycled commuted the 60 miles in. I'm on my pride and joy. My Ribble R872 carbon roadbike. Looking sharp, anthracite frame (anthracite is just a way to make grey sound less boring), but with bright green bar tape to give it some style. Riding in was alright. Struggled physically more than I expected. But I attributed that to having to lug a heavy laptop in, plus the heat around midday. It was good to get some practice in in the heat, as the Berlin trip had been really mild for May. Was it alright? I hate riding into London, the suburbs just stretch on forever. And navigating London traffic and pedestrians really is a wild, wild west nowadays. Feels like Vietnam, a complete free-for-all, nobody obeying road rules, whoevers boldest gets to go. But I made it there in one piece.

Did some work from the office. Went for drinks. I took my bike to the drinks, an outdoorsy bar near London Bridge. It was broad daylight, with many, many people milling around. Many people. So it felt like a completely fine place to lock the bike up. It was with a D-lock, the wheels were not quick-release. What are they gonna nick? Drinks were fun. I didn't get too smashed knowing I had a massive ride on Saturday. It's nice drinking a reasonable amount, having a good time, going home, sleeping decently, waking up feeling fresh(ish). Can tell I'm getting old xD. I go to unlock my bike so I can cycle back to St Panc. Erm…there's no handlebars. Why's there no handlebars? Hmmmm. That's awkward. Someone had snipped the brake cables and knicked the handlebars plus cables. In broad daylight. With so many people around. London…sigh. This is my only road bike by the way. I'm both angry and embarrassed. Close to tears. Feeling very foolish having to drag my bike carcass onto the tube. To make matters worse the train from Londton Bridge to St Panc is delayed. I end up sprinting with it across St Panc…all to just miss my train by seconds. None for another hour. Full of rage and negative emotions. Lock my bike up to go to the toilet and get some food. The railway person informs me I can't do that and they'll call security if I walk off. I am so not in the mood. I really don't care. I inform the railway person how much I don't care. I hold up my hands in the "ah, what can ya' do?" style pose. And just walk off. Currently seething pretty hardcore, but events like this only increase my resolve…if there was any doubt as to whether I'd make it before, now the doubt is gone. I'm probably going to have to do this on my hybrid. But nothing is gonna stop me doing the 250miles. Almost certainly won't get there for sunset, might be rolling in at 1am, but fuck it. I'm not letting this shit day stop me. I will channel this feeling into my feet on Saturday.

Friday morning is phoning up every bike shop around Canterbury. Explaining the situation over and over. Asking the impossible. The Bike Warehouse in Faversham tells me they can always give it a go, but no promises. There's nothing to lose, might as well go with a maybe rather than a no.

I drop the bike off there at about 10am, at which point it goes on the stand. It's internal cabling, and all 4 cables have been cut and need replacing. Not a simple job. But magically the bike is sorted at 4:30pm, 30 mins before closing time. It has cost me a ridiculous sum for brand new shifters, I have no insurance, but I'm still elated that they've turned it around. The 250mile battle against the sun has been salvaged! I really am so very grateful to the mechanics at TheBikeWarehouse in Faversham for doing everything to turn it around in the nick of time 🙇

Saturday morning: Alarm blares at about 3am. Eurgh. Genuine chance I turn off the alarm and bin the attempt before it's even started. But it would be so silly to bail after all the bike stress. So after a couple of minutes when the backup alarm goes off, I roll out of bed. Eat my overnight oats: Today a mix of porridge, obviously, milk, yoghurt, honey, cinnamon, walnuts, cranberries, chia seeds, all the good shiz. Plus smashing a quick coffee. So in general I shy away from caffeine during the early stages of long rides. Because I avoid caffeine in day-to-day life, my tolerance stays low. So a double-espresso literally transforms me into a viking beserker. This is great late on, but going into berserker-mode too early uses up too much energy. However I'll usually start with a coffee just to get into it. When it kicks in as my body is finishing its warmup, I can push on and it lets me set a fast baseline tempo for the ride. Between sips I pull on my gear, fill my special shorts pockets with a full loaf of cinnamon and fruit bread sandwiches (filled with honey and peanut butter), and then my homemade flapjack...which as usual has not held itself together at all, and is just a crumbly bag of dry porridge. Out the door and into the crisp summer morning. It's an eerie feeling riding down Hengist Way Ramsgate-bound, in the pre-dawn dark, on what is essentially a dual carriageway at 3:30am with not a car around.

People defecate on Ramsgate a lot. Figuratively and literally. But Ramsgate harbour, with its flotilla of small boats is a lovely view and way to kick off the challenge. I stop, have a quick nutrigrain bar, snap some selfies of me with the Eastern dawn shoreline, then it's off...back the exact same way we came. Now in the dawn twilight.

On the way back the way I came, around Sturry, which funnily enough is basically the outskirts of Canterbury, where I live...I feel something off with the rear of the bike. Is that a puncture? Feels like a puncture? I stop. Yep, it's not a massive one, but the tyre is definitely going down.

No problemo. These things happen. I've got plenty of spare tubes. Easy peasy. I take off the wheel, fully deflate the tyre. I go to put a little air into the new tube to fit it easier......err where's my pump? I check the big frame bag on the bike. Nope. Check my back pockets. Nope. Check the frame bag again. Getting a bit anxious now. Nope. Take literally everything out of my pockets in-case it's lurking in the depths somewhere. Nope. FFS. In the chaos of the previous day, I've somehow left my pump at home. There's no way to fix this puncture, and it's 5:15 AM, nowhere open.

Am I close enough to home to run back there? Probably. That'll be the last resort. Writing this back in hindsight, I realise I could have probably called a taxi. But I tend to forget that taxis exist as a concept. Up until a friend came to visit me in Canterbury last month, I'd genuinely taken about 10 taxis in my lifetime.

What a waste of money. Just walk ¯_(ツ)_/¯. So instead I call my mum, apologised profusely for waking her up so early, and beg for a lift back to my house. She agrees, so long as she has time to have a coffee first. I can't really say no. In the time it takes her to reach me, I've genuinely walked a third of the way back to my house xD But it was still appreciated.

Found the pump in my house, but decide to completely change the front tyre. If it had punctured once, good chance it's near the end of life and will happen again.

I wonder whether I should cycle back to the spot where I got picked up….but I'd already technically cycled the stretch between puncture pickup and my house...just in the wrong direction. So in my head this didn't violate the coast to coast ride. And the total mileage would still hit 250. Plus it's my own silly little challenge, so I can make and bend the rules however I want! So out the house I went, very relieved that I'd got a lift back. A bit apprehensive about how much time had been lost. Probably about 45 minutes. To make it before sunset I don't really have time to hang around. There's not going to be time for a lunch stop, or more mechanicals.

I smashed it out of Canterbury along one of the main A-roads towards Charing. A fun 40 mph descent of Charing Hill to get the adrenaline flowing and Westwards we continued.

There were some great forest roads around Guildford and Dorking. Riding on my own for the most part. The weather was warm but not too warm. A spot of cloud cover meaning I didn't need to be vigilantly creaming myself every hour.

The going was really good. Staying around 16mph on the flats. I was pretty fucking fired up after the theft, and felt like I could and would push myself to the limit.

No stop for lunch. Even if I technically had the time I'd still vote against a long lunch stop. If you're having a nice chilled long ride, then a long lunch stop is fine. But when you're smashing it, and you really need to push yourself, lunch is the enemy. If you stop for more than about 20 minutes your body starts going into recovery mode, and it's difficult to get it going again. So if your body is feeling good around lunchtime, don't stop. There's a risk that afterwards you're going to inexplicably feel miserable. Keep going until your body is pretty much forcing you to stop is my motto. Breaks in general are frowned upon. When you do big rides with other people (e.g. audaxes, which are like "unofficial" really long road "races" [which 80% of people don't take as a serious race])...you notice that you can fly by someone doing 2mph less than you. 2mph is a lot for a bicycle...but then when you stop for a quick piss, there they are, trundling back past you. The best way to cover really long distances fast is to just limit stops. Don't stop unless absolutely necessary. Eat on the go. Drink on the go. If you're a pro rider, even piss on the go. I do not have the bike-handling or penis-handling skills for that. Try to never stop for a single reason. Combine suncream, excretion, grabbing extra supplies, everything into a single stop. Prioritise supplies from petrol stations or small, fast shops, rather than sit-down cafes.

The ride is going perfectly. I'm totally on top of nutrition and hydration. But things take a bit of a turn at a small bakery in Bramley, a little village north of Basingstoke, almost halfway across the country. There's a level-crossing, and I just miss making it before the barriers come down. So this is a good time to stock up on extra food and water in the bakery next door.

As I'm speed-wolfing my tuna sandwich and coke, I get talking to a large, cheery gentlemen in there. He knows about the chase-the-sun from the hundreds of cyclists who descended upon him last weekend. He's very enthusiastic about my attempt, and as I'm leaving, he grabs a pack of two Belgian buns off the shelf and just hands them to me. Score! So I assume he owned the place. He must have owned the place. Otherwise he's just some random bloke, who conned me into shoplifting, but whatever, nobody objected

The buns are absolutely flipping massive. The size of your outstretched hand. And real depth to them. If I put a bra on and stuffed one into each cup you would be incredibly aroused. Gigantic! They won't fit even into my special pockets, so I try to nibble one down to size. I'm very grateful for the gift, too grateful to just bin them...but Belgian buns are kind of awkward cycling snacks. The sticky icing gets everywhere. You end up with sticky bars, sticky brakes, sticky everything. So I end up deciding to power through both of them, and then I can wipe my hands properly once. As opposed to constant grazing and having permanently sticky fingers for the whole ride. But they were so massive, and I'd just finished a sandwich and a flapjack...so my stomach groaned at its fullness. I'd eaten too much, whilst trying to still go too hard. My blood sugar spiked from the buns and flapjack. My blood sugar crashed. When your blood sugar sinks too low, it actually makes you feel a bit sick and decreases your appetite. Which is really fucking bad if you still have over 100 miles left to cycle and kind of need to be eating food for fuel.

So the 2nd leg of the journey is a bit of a bonky-haze. The early afternoon heat was also not helping. The Southern coast-to-coast comes out as harder than it looks on paper due to the route profile. More of the hills come at the start of the second half, in the North Wessex Downs, and they come on bullshit backlane country roads. These roads are filled with gravel. They're never wide enough for a bike and car to safely pass each other. Blind bends galore. Therefore every downhill has to be taken at a snails pace to stay safe, whilst your average speed is hit massively by the upward bits.

At this point, it's also early-mid afternoon. The heat is at its highest. You're sweating a lot and losing water plus electrolytes. With my strategy of stopping as little as possible. I end up running out of water, as these sections have very few villages with pubs or shops. When I eventually stumble across a bikers pub, the small, black stones in the gravel car-park swim slightly in my vision. I try to down an ice-cold pint of coke and get brain-freeze. But at least my bottles are filled and don't have to worry about water for a while. Also I'd have preferred a small shop to a pub. Pubs don't really have sugary snacks. But I was too thirsty and just had to stop at the next available place with liquid.

Several minutes later, now hydrated, but still a bit out of it...I'm trying to eat a flapjack on an empty piece of road, focusing on extracting the flapjack from my pockets a bit too hard...I manage to ride straight off the road and into a deep ditch at the side of it. Somehow I "stay upright". I end up doing a big endo at the bottom of the ditch but don't fall off. A close shave, and I am much more careful eating and drinking further along.

There's another pub further on where I never consciously decided to stop. But out of my control I feel myself pulling over, downing some more coke and some salty crisps. You really start to crave salty, savoury stuff like crisps and sausage rolls and semen towards the end of massive rides.

But as per usual when you're floundering on these mega-rides and feel like you've hit bottom...If you just "ride it out" (get it?). Just keep pedalling....your body, well my body at least, recovers from what food you did get and it suddenly becomes easier again at some point. Mentally the ride is always great after this point of recovery. After pushing through the bad times, the remainder of the ride is very zen. It does feel a bit like how your brain responds to coming out of a psychedelic trip.

Around the stage where I'm hitting the zen recovery zone, I remember there's an absolute Lamborghini Countach of a hill at one stage. But I also remember it being the last major hurdle, and not that far from the finish. Forgotten the name, but it does leap up to nearly 20 mph. I do my pedal dancing up it, surprising myself at how I'm doing. Feels great at the top, the toughest hill in the bag. After the Berlin adventure, no offence to San, but I'm really savouring my Ribble. Feeling like a proper cyclist, smoothly stroking my legs round. Getting down low. Feeling the speed.

I start to see signs for Cheddar and know I'm close. Cheddar Gorge is less than 20 miles from the beach finish. But I can see the sun low on the skyline before me. I have no idea when the actual sunset is, and it's already gone 7pm. The zen period is over. I start to panic, and respond by going pretty full-blast, thinking that every second might count.

Cheddar gorge should be a fun, flowing, fast, scenic descent. Steep rocks on either side. Fantastic bends. But my mind is blorged. And I am barely with it enough to be dodging all the dodgy hazards the gorge brings. Massive incident causing rocks that fall and end up in the middle of the road. And not a problem last year, but this year the stupid sheep. Their new hobby seems to be hanging out and congregating on blind bends right in your path.

I'm still through the gorge and the town of Cheddar in the blink of an eye. Adrenaline up from trying not to crash at this late stage. Can I see the coast from here? I can't remember, I think so, but it's only about another 10 miles. I'm still pushing it, not knowing how long I have left.

It transpires that in summer, it just takes a really fucking long time for the sun to set. This doesn't seem very romantic. It's just sets boringly slow. If you want a romantic sunset, wait for winter. But I'm happy with that, it means I make it to the beach and promenade around 8-something PM. The sun still technically there, just hidden behind the clouds.

Ah, I've done it. Being an unofficial chase-the-sun day there's no fanfare, or other cyclists milling around. So I just saunter along the beach, wallowing in the nice personal feeling of having completed it. I beat the sun. Smashed my longest ride record. And did it all after not knowing if I had a bike to do it on the day before.

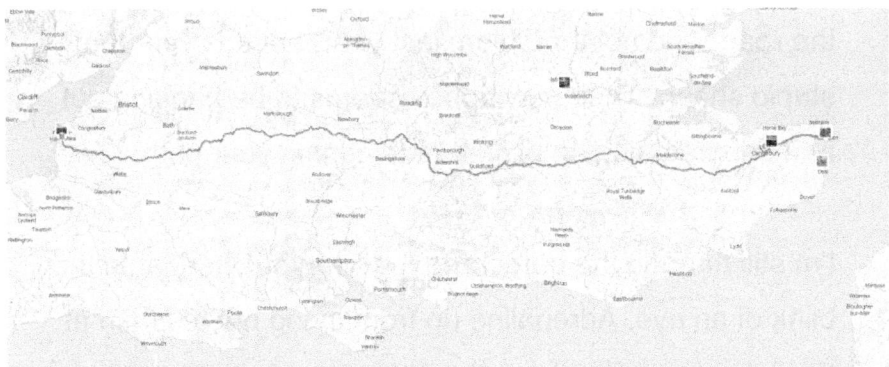

The hotel room is fine, I rifle through the draws because I'm just curious and bored. You'd expect to just drop asleep after something like this. But I find the opposite happens. The day has been so mentally intense that it can be hard to drop off and sleep soundly. So I'm rifling through the drawers. There's underwear in the drawers. Interesting. I wonder if it's clean, as I don't actually have any underwear with me due to being in cycling gear. I smell it. I regret smelling it. Apart from the used underwear, the hotel is pleasant.

In the morning I try to work out how to get home. Probably should have planned that earlier but oh well. Great Western trains want you to book a bicycle space, I try and do this online but fail and give up. They'd probably be fine if I just turned up...but I'm in a weird mood. After doing multiple hard days on the Berlin trip, I wonder if I can do another fairly big ride today. So instead of training it the whole way home, I can do an 85 mile ride from Weston-super-mare to Andover, where I can get a different train operator, which doesn't need bike reservations.

It means I get to go up cheddar gorge in the reverse

direction. Nice to actually enjoy it. Well...I'm going uphill with pretty battered legs and burning lungs so it's not as enjoyable as I'd expected. In hindsight I should have got off and walked up it. But hindsight is 50/50. Going through the gorge I grabbed some gorge-ous (ha....ha....ha) fudge. One box as presents for the bike shop. One as a present to my mum for 5am pickup. They get absolutely obliterated in my pockets. Both crushed from lack of space, and inevitably melted from sweaty, body heat. What a great gift they'll make ☺. After I'm properly warmed up and into it, my legs are actually all-right the day after. It's the usual "stiff when you start", but they loosen up as you get into it. It's mainly my arse that is struggling and so I have to keep jumping out of the saddle just to give it a bit of relief.

I've never been to Stonehenge. Turns up my route to Andover went right past it...but I forgot to look at it. I did wonder why there was a bus-stop called "Stonehenge" ⬚. It would also simultaneously cool and alarming riding over Salisbury plains. Filled with warning signs for gun ranges and live firing, and roadsigns asking you to look out for tanks crossing. All-in-all a pretty interesting and worthwhile ride. Didn't see any tanks though. Or get shot at. Disappointing.

Interlude 2: Kevin

Hi, I'm raising money for my friend Kevin. Here's the link. Please donate generously. He was on the last train home from a night out in London. Yes we'd sank a few too many pints watching the six nations, but he still did nothing wrong. He was just having a harmless vape on the train, when the nazi of a conductor bellowed at Kevin that he couldn't vape in here. And if he continued, he'd be kicked off at the next station. Fucking ridiculous. Kevin, being someone who cares deeply about right and wrong, and also being 12 pints deep, stood his ground. Didn't let the fucker bully him. Good for Kevin. For too long have we been treated like second-class citizens. But then you know what happened? The bloody bastard went and actually kicked him off. In the middle of nowhere. Unbelievable. Well he didn't technically kick him, but he said he was phoning the police and Kevin feels like a criminal record could hamper his career prospects if he ever wants to move stateside. But still, how bloody dare he! Vaping is a FUNDAMENTAL human right! When are people going to realise this?!

He had to take a late-night taxi the whole way home, cost him nearly £200! Fortunately he's one of the most promising junior chartered accountants of his generation. But imagine if he wasn't one of the most promising junior chartered accounts of his generation? Imagine if he was working class? Imagine if he wasn't white? He would have had to sleep on a bench in Ashford of all places! The horror! So if we can just raise £200 to cover Kevin's taxi, after his outrageous treatment, and standing up for all us vapists, it'll be most appreciated. **Vape 4 Kevin**!

Netherlands With the Boys

I'm gonna be brutally honest. This is the most mundane trip of the year to read about. I'm quite keen on my friends, and would like them to stay my friends. Hence I am loathe to bring them aboard my insane pain train. Turning them against both me, and cycling as a hobby in general. So this was a fairly chill trip. Therefore I'll make it a short chapter (**editor note**: With the amount you waffle, is that possible?).

So let's blitz it. In July, me and a couple of long-time programming and gaming friends arranged to go gallivanting around the Dutch countryside for a few days. Our basecamp is a Europarcs just outside the Hoge de Veluwe national park. We'll do daily rides out in each direction. Europarcs is essentially European Centreparcs...but half the price. If you can get enough friends to share a chalet it's great value for money...technically it's more of an elaborate hut than a chalet, but it's close enough.

Neither of my friends are "experienced" cyclists. That's doing them a bit of a disservice. They've both ridden bikes a lot. But as normal, everyday type people. They're not wearing skint-tight aero clothes, or obsessing over how many grams they can shave off with their new carbon wheels. There's Christian,. Christian lives on the outskirts of Manchester and has been doing fairly substantial rides around the hills, or over to Liverpool. Blonde goatee with glasses. Used to be…not big big, but bigger. But seems to have lost a noticeable amount of weight since I last saw him, so looks like the long days out cycling are working for him (After big rides I personally tend to over-indulge, building up bad food habits which take days or even weeks to kick…although it's become a lot easier since I've gone vegan and everything tasty or calorie-dense seems off-menu ☺. If only the Cardamom & Pistachio Buns from the local Fringe & Ginge coffee shop weren't so amazing!). Then there's Dave. Dave is leaner with curly black hair. The oldest of us 3 I think. Or at least he looks old. Sorry Dave. I mean older than me and Christian. Not old, old. Anyway Dave used to commute by bike a lot, but apparently hasn't cycled outside of popping to the shops in a loooong time. So how was he going to fare? The initial plan had been to ride from Brussels to Amsterdam. But as with any cycling trip, there were unanswered questions about how to get the bikes there and back. Flying with a bike is a faff if you don't do it regularly. Eurostar to anywhere other than Brussels is a faff disassembling bikes. I was hot on the idea of just riding out there. They were not so hot.

In the end, after I confidently claim that "*The Netherlands is pancake flat. Did you know I'm somewhat of an expert on The Netherlands. I've consumed copious amounts of their drugs*". So on paper, it doesn't matter what bike you're on if there's no hills. Even on an old banger, we can cruise around at 12mph, eventually getting to where we're going. So we opt for the super-simple-solution of renting Omafiets directly from Europarcs. Dutch city bikes. Literally translates to Granny-bike I believe. Nothing fancy. Heavy as a rhino. But perfectly suitable for getting around a flat country. Pretty similar to my Berlin bike (might actually be an Omafiets).

I'm going to head out there a couple of days beforehand. Multiple reasons really. I've managed to avoid flying for a long time, and Arnhem is close enough I can technically get there without flying. But it would be a long and arduous mix of cycling, trains and ferries. So it makes it more pleasant to stop off halfway, break the trip in two. The other bonus: it gives me the chance of a magic mushroom day to myself. Neither of my friends seem keen on them. I've never really understood how people who pour pints of literal poison into themselves on a daily basis, can be so resistant to the much healthier mushrooms? Although I imagine people build up this idea that you have to have a high dose and be tripping balls. When really that's like judging alcohol by assuming the only way to drink it is to just down whole bottles of vodka.

Although to balance out my support, you really should check out Hallucinogen Persisting Perception Disorder (HPPD) before deciding to blow your brain with hallucinogens. Sort of the "flashbacks" people talk about. But not really. Less intense than a proper flashback, but if you have it constantly...hence the persistent part...I imagine it sucks pretty hard. Now I'm no longer a man of science, although I do still look in the toilet afterwards and make a mental note of where I am on the Bristol Stool chart...but based on the papers I've skim-read, it feels like the chances of HPPD are likely to be proportional to the strength of the hallucinations. Which is why I feel perfectly comfortable taking a lowish-medium dose of Atlantis truffles each time. Enough to change the way you think and your perceptions...but not so much that your brain starts inventing things which aren't actually there. Again I stress, do your own research and only do what you feel comfortable with. Especially as some people might be more genetically perceptible to HPPD. Plus if your head's in a bad place and you want mushrooms to dig you out of it, you're rolling a dice. Mushrooms might help immensely, but they might also dig you deeper into the hole. Hopefully in the future therapists will be able to do guided trips with patients to help direct the tripee. But we don't live in the future at the moment.

Where was I before I went on a mushroom tangent? Oh yeah, friends not into them. But I'm also not keen on prodding friends into trying them anyway. The last two times I've done mushrooms with friends, someone has vomited and had a not nice time. Advice: Bring an empty carrier bag with you just in-case, and don't fight it. If you're feeling nauseous, just chill and sit on the nearest bench. It will pass. If it doesn't. If you start to taste that weird, wet, metallicy taste...you're past the point of no return. Don't fight it. Pull your hair back. Get the bag ready. And once it's up it's up. You're not going to have a strong trip, but you'll be feeling OK.

So...I'm done with tangents I promise. I decide that I'll stop off in Breda en-route. Why Breda? Well why not Breda? I've already been to so many random places in the Netherlands that it's tough to find new ones to explore. It looks like there's some nice countryside on the outskirts to get lost in. It has a smartshop to buy some magic truffles to enhance said countryside. It sounds a bit like Bread….. ¯_(ツ)_/¯. Off to ~~Bread~~Breda it is!

I'm on my bright blue Dahon Mariner folding bike. Basically a budget brompton. For people interested in a folding bike, I'd recommend you try out riding, folding and carrying one before committing to it. First time on it it felt like I was 10 years old again, riding my little sister's bike around the garden, pretending to be Valentino Rossi. You get used to that a bit, but I'd still opt for renting a proper bike if I'm going to be doing big rides where I'm heading. Plus if you don't splash out for the super-lightweight ones, it's a pretty hefty beast to lug around when folded. If you have a cyclist's upper body physique you will Struggle. No offence to Chris Froome, but if the Tour de France had been done on folding bikes he would be fucked.

The trip starts like Berlin, I get myself down to Dover and on the ferry to Dunkerque like I've done so many times before. Again nobody checks my bags. At this point I actually want to get stopped and searched, just to remove the temptation of becoming a wealthy international drugs smuggler. I still have my highly explosive can of GT-85 for a hacky chain clean and lube job. That gets through again. The reason for the folding bike comes into play in Belgium. It's a chilled 90 minute cycle from Dunkerque to Adinkerke, the home of Plopsaland, the famous and funnily-named theme park. The ride isn't perfect. Bloody clacking sound and gears jumping around. I blame the jokers at where I bought the bike from, who didn't index the gears properly in the slightest, and I'm too scared to make the situation worse mid-trip. But it's a nice sunny day through Northern France and Belgium, and there's no schedule or deadline. And from Adinkerke I hop onto a train, having to change at Ghent and Antwerp, eventually finding my way to Breda.

I arrive in Breda early evening. A very non-descript Dutch town. Couldn't pick it out of a police lineup. A bit like my testicles. Once late at night in St Pancras, a man asked me to describe my testicles. Like I said, couldn't pick them out of a police lineup. Best conversation ever. Breda: There's Dutch buildings. Lots of bicycles. Pleasant. But no reason to visit as a tourist. At all. Nothing you can claim is wrong with it. But there are so many other places in the world to visit. I collect the magic truffles en-route to the hotel, the hotel lying on the edge of the city. Right up against the forest and countryside I mentioned, so that you can walk out your door and straight into it. The room is medium-strength green. Kind of old décor. Reminds me of The Shining. Would be nice, if not for the blood-spattered corpses dotting the walls. Probably should have seen that one coming. It's lying right on the edge of the forest, in an area known to be a bit marshy. Bloody mosquitoes. I add to the collection late in the evening. The gigantic blood splatter indicating I've probably already been got. This should have been a warning about how the trip would transpire tomorrow. But alas I ignored it.

I get up nice and early. No breakfast. You shouldn't eat big before mushrooms. Use my keys to slice open the vacuum sealed pack of earthy, solid blobs. Crack open my bar of 99% dark chocolate, and get to work. Truffles are not a pleasant drug to consume. Technically magic mushrooms are illegal in the Netherlands. But truffles are….are they the underground part of the mushroom? Think so. These parts are legal. They still contain psilocybin, just in lower doses. So you need to eat much more. 10 or 15 grams does not sound like a lot. But it is a lot when they taste like what can only be described as "old mud". So dark chocolate is my way of masking the terrible flavour. I can't stand dark chocolate anyway, so it's not like it can psychologically "ruin" the flavour. Unlike the way triple-vodka and cokes at uni ruined drinking straight coke for a few years. Straight coke just tasted like bad decisions, future-vomit and blinding headaches. Some people make mushroom tea; that feels like a faff to me. I've also tried soaking them in lemon juice. That seemed alright as well, but you need to have some way of grinding and mixing them.

So I suck it up, and chew it up, munching away for a good 15 minutes. Not going too fast and making myself feel sick. I swallow the last bit, brush my teeth, check my backpack and head out into the woods. It's supposed to be the middle of the summer, but this summer has been pretty atrocious weather-wise in the UK, and it seems the Netherlands have been getting the same treatment as well. It's closer to a swamp than woods at times.

Shoes are getting filthy, but no worries. Mushrooms are kicking in. I don't have much of a plan. Just walk from one end of the woods to the other. See what happens. On most trips my brain will be buzzing with fresh new thoughts, they often seem either revelatory or hilarious at the time, but are usually just kinda weird: "*Everything will be alright, just DON'T EAT THE BEES!*" is one I remember in Rotterdam's botanical gardens, when noticing the gate in the waist-high fence to the beehive field had been left often. Can be useful though, as we, or at least I, tend to overcomplicate life. And on mushrooms I'm pretty sure you're not smarter. Pretty sure you're dumber. But sometimes looking at things from a dumb perspective clarifies things. It's basically for therapy for people who can't be fucked with NHS waiting lists.

Mushrooms also amplify your experiences and emotions...so the main thing I'm getting so far from this trip is: "I'm so bloody drained dude. My bones are tired". So my brain is not buzzing around, working through things, or tickling my funny bone. On this trip it's simply AWOL. Whether it's from the accumulation of all the cycling, climbing and other activities I do. Or the travelling from the day before. Or the poor sleep from mosquito induced paranoia: "*Is there one in the room with me? Is that a shadow or a bug?*". Whatever it is, my brain is telling me: "*I'm pretty much done here. You can walk into the woods. Do what you want for the next couple of hours. But I'm off. I'm having a waking nap. Good luck without me*". This isn't even Mr Conscious handing over control to Mr Lizard. They're both napping. I am just zombie.

So I trudge on. Like a soldier, exhausted from combat, being ordered to move from one position to another, for a reason he does not understand, and does not care about anymore. After some more trudging I finally realise that all I want to do is just stop. Stop and pause. When was the last time I just paused and looked at a tree? For like, several minutes; and just appreciated it, and noticed all the details. I want nothing more than to just cease this endless, aimless march forwards, and just chill with a tree. But deep down I know if I do that...then the mozzies will come. I remember at the time I felt like this was a metaphor for modern life in general:
- The mosquitoes are the forces of capitalism.
- Modern society forces us to keep moving forwards.
- Sometimes we want to just pause for a bit, look at a tree for a while.
- For how long? Dunno. It would be nice to just pause until we don't feel like it anymore. Maybe minutes. Maybe months
- But as soon as you take a pause:
  - Landlord: "*Where's the rent money?*"
  - Resource companies: "*Where's the electrical money?*"

- Older people: "*Why aren't you investing in your pension plan? If you don't you won't be able to travel the world when your body is too broken and battered to enjoy it anyway*"
- These are like the mosquitoes
- Draining you. Draining your blood as you just try to chill and regroup. Reset yourself in life. Regain your footing.

But what about holidays? Isn't that what they're for? A break from this constant need for "do-ing" and productivity. But how many holiday days do you get? And can you bring yourself to "waste" them just by taking some days off to regroup. For someone like me, even travelling is stressful. Dealing with airports, getting to things on-time. And I've never been a "sit-on-the-beach" type of person, so holidays are often more tiring than work. (editor note: hmmm. Interesting. Maybe I should just take some days off at home next year. And not consider them a waste. Do less mental challenges. This is one of the good things about writing. I wouldn't have thought about that and changed anything. So if you're still reading and enjoying this…I think I've just talked myself out of doing a sequel. Maybe one year on, one year off for the mental stuff?).

And then even if you do have a truly relaxing holiday. Is it enough? It takes days for you to unwind. And then when you finally think: "*Oh, I'm actually chilled out. I'd forgotten what it was like to not have chronic low-level stresses.....aaaaand I'm flying home tomorrow*". Although that's actually one of my favourite benefits and uses of mushrooms. They can often transport you directly into that end-of-holiday chill-zone, do not pass Go. This gives you more days of proper relaxation on the rest of your holiday. Well that's the "plan"....

But back to the present. There's supposedly a nice, pretty raised wooden walkway at some point. I never make it there. I hadn't noticed mozzies on the outskirts (except the couple in my room), but the deeper I get, the more they multiply. I try to just keep moving and hope they can't hit a moving target. But they can. I'm getting eaten alive. Not the best way to chillax. A walking bed and breakfast for the forest. I bet the mozzies can't believe their luck, me walking in this early in the morning with my sweet, tasty blood. Looking around, I am incredulous at all the shorts and t-shirt wearing Dutch people, out for a relaxing weekend stroll. Somehow oblivious, or immune, to the absolute suckfest I am currently enduring deep in these woods. Eventually I tell myself enough is enough. I'm fucking done. When one lands on my ear with a high-pitched whine I turn the opposite direction, and literally run for it. Not jog. Run. I run and run and run. Only stopping when I get to a small clearing, with some nice duck-bearing-ponds. The path is narrow here and I don't want to freak out the Dutch families, bowling through them with my saucer eyes. There's a tiny newt, smaller than my little finger. Playing dead, standing stock-still in the middle of what seems quite a busy path. Pretty sure he's going to get squished, but he was cute whilst he lived. I walk on, the background blur noise of cars growing stronger. I'm reaching civilization. Woohoo! Fuck nature! No more running for now,my body naturally untenses as I get closer and closer towards Breda.

Phew. I am out of the woods. Quite literally. I pass a cafe on Breda outskirts. After my ordeal I feel like treating myself to something, so I stop. I treat myself to tomato soup. That doesn't sound like a treat, but trust me. With some good bread, and this is good bread, it's divine bread, with some good bread a bowl of soup can be great comfort food. (**editor note**: And it's healthy. Why the fuck haven't I had a bowl of soup in months? Why am I not eating soup all the time? New Years resolution: Eat Soup!).

As the soup hits the back of my mouth I'm transported through space and time. No, it's not the drugs. It's the power of memories. So often whilst growing up, at the weekend I would be in front of the TV, watching Formula 1 or maybe a 2nd round FA cup tie at some rinky-dink ground in a tiny town. And my Mum would make just simple Heinz tinned tomato soup with some buttery toast. The warmness fills and spreads through my body. Tastes pretty good too. Somehow forty percent of it does end up down my top, note: maybe don't wear a white top whilst tripping, but I am in food nirvana and zero fucks are given. The shirt is a worthy sacrifice to experience this meal. I finish and then just chill here for a while. Regrouping; ensuring the terror has fully subsided. It's nice to be able to finish eating in a restaurant for once, and just sit there relaxed. Not have my mind cycling through what I'm going to do next, where I'm going to go. When are they going to bring the check? C'mon c'mon, I've got places to be, people to do. Let's go Let's go!.....None of that now. Just calm. This is the "end of holiday" vibes I aforementioned. Ahhhhh. (editor note: I have a wide relaxed smile right now just remembering this :))

From here on out it is a pretty pleasant remainder of the trip. Sauntering through Breda, listening to some good tunes. Having a proper headbang on a random bench when the good bit of "When the Levee Breaks" kicks in (Led Zep). Found a nice park....with no mosquitoes. I watch the ducks in the lake and the ripples they generate, even whilst apparently stationary. The way all those ripples collide with the other ducks ripples and form new wave-patterns. Very cool. Probably a metaphor in there somewhere if you want to go digging. But I'm just enjoying watching the ripples. As a child I was very into fluid dynamics. Loved just watching streams and stuff. Dunno why I ignored that stuff in physics in favour of boring subatomic particles and black holes. Not boring...but I would literally spend 20 minute staring at a stream. When was the last time I spent 20 minutes staring at a black hole? Probably too egotistical and that seemed like the hard stuff...but really anything chaotic is proper mental. I dunno where I'm going here...

There's lots of rental-app scooters in Breda, a bit like Lime bikes, but proper petrol scooters. Like mopeds, not like the piddly e-scooters. I'm walking down an outer-town housey-road, at a crossroads, with no-one else about...when I spot a scooter lying sadly on its side, handlebars askew, half in the dirt of a flower bed. As I walk past it, I think about how sad it looks. I'm reminded of The Good Samaritan. Or Batman. Someone should do something. Is it any of my business? Not really. It's not my town. I'm never gonna ride this scooter. But I've stopped by now, and It'll literally take less time to sort it out, than this internal discussion on the moral action is taking in my head. So I just go and right it. Put it on its stand. It looks much happier now. I'm well chuffed with myself. I'm not the hero Breda asked for. But I'm the hero it's got right now. I am a hero! Superpower: picking up injured mopeds.

I perform a one-eighty spin to carry on with my walk. Over the other side of the street is another scooter. This one is literally upside down. WTF Breda. It does not even look physically possible, looks like a glitch in a videogame. I chuckle and shake my head, and keep on moving.

I've forgotten what happened for the rest of the day. Not much probably. More reading. I'd been reading "Sorrow and Bliss" by...somebody. Best fiction book I've read in donkeys. So I was content reading my book, Breda didn't exactly seem like it was going to be party-central, and the main thing I'd learnt from my trip was: My body needs rest, and a nice quiet night in would do it grand.

After my trip of terror and tribulations, it's onto Arnhem the next day. Just a short direct train from Breda there. Still megatired though. It was hard to sleep with swollen insect bites. Kept awake by the itch. But hopefully I've finally learnt my lesson. This isn't the first time it has happened either. *"Oooh, I like the woods. I'll have a nice walk in the woods. That'll be nice won't it. Ooooh, I'm being eaten alive. I forgot the woods contained beings that ate humans. Silly me!"*. I am now about 32 times bitten, which would be about 4,294,967,296 times shy by my calculations. So hopefully that's the last time. I'll stick to tripping in Het Zwin on the coast, where the mosquitoes cannot deal with the high winds. A smooth train and then it's a short 20 minute cycle from Arnhem to the Europarcs above it. Oh and it turns out literally above it, not just North, gravitationally upwards. Uh-oh. My promise of "pancake-flat" is looking a bit shaky. I grind up two pretty chunky hills through the woods to reach it. Whoops. Sorry guys. They're not massive hills, but when you're on a shite bike, any hill is a hill. The cycling we have in store might be less straightforward than I'd anticipated...

I meet the guys at Europarcs, we were cheeky and manage to collect the bikes the night before we'd booked them. So we get a bonus evening ride in. As the bikes were unlocked for us, Christian and Dave laugh as I adjust my saddle to a reasonable height. Erm...ok :| I narrow my eyes but they seem to be serious. They leave their saddles alone. It takes one day for one of them to be complaining of knee pain. Yes I am a smug and arrogant bellend when it comes to saddle height :)

So out we head for a "short-ish" loop around the outskirts of the main national park bit. Dave had forgotten to bring a helmet, or sunglasses, or anything useful for cycling at all. Christian had brought correct gear (although we had different definitions of "cycling shorts". To me if they're not padded, they're not "cycling shorts". So I would end up the only person with an intact groin and a functioning arse by the end of the trip).

Christian had been the driving force in the group chat, posting messages like: "*Not long to go now guys. C'mon, time to get some training in*!", along with pics of him on his bike in the Peak District. My cycling addiction means I lie to friends and family about how much I actually cycle, to try and seem "relatively normal", so I had just kept quiet, but knew the trip would never trouble me. Dave….didn't seem like he could be bothered with training or preparation. But who could blame him, after all, it *should* have been all flat.

I'd never ridden bikes with Dave or Christian before. Turns out Christian was a serious spurter. Can I elaborate? OK. He had a very "interesting" cycling style. He would furiously smash the pedals for several seconds, putting out some tremendous watts, leaving us in the dust…..for 2.3 seconds, but then he would attempt to coast and freewheel for the next 15 seconds to recover. This would have been fine on his home bike, probably low weight and well-maintained drive-train….but not on this decrepit granny bike:

- Weighing in at surely over 15kg
- With a drivetrain that has probably had years of outdoor neglect
- Wheels with the rolling resistance of a hedgehog
- and to top it all off: a front wheel dynamo to power an unnecessarily bright headlight, which completely sapped any remaining power.

Literally as soon as you stopped pedalling, the bike would grind to a halt within metres.

The spurty style is quite literally impossible on these bikes.

Which is awkward, as clearly Christian's body had self-optimised for this style of cycling. An absurd style yes, but his style nonetheless. A gentle, consistent cadence just didn't seem to be in his inventory. Most of the time we were on false-flat up or down. Riding for miles along an empty, straight path, many trees on our right. Sort of nice. But they were also the kind of regimentedly planted trees that feel a bit human and artificial. Inside the park is a lot nicer.

As our 30km loop around the park drew on he started to struggle and was hanging off the back on the slight uphills. But these were barely uphills, and this proving a challenge did not bode well for the rest of the trip.

First full day. Enthusiasm was not dampened by the shitty bikes or the shitty weather forecast. Dry when we set out, but an ominous afternoon ahead. Our plan for the day was to ride to Emmerich and back, a town in Germany, the first town over the border from us. I had been hyping up German bakeries to the max after the Berlin trip, especially the Bienenstich (German for bee-sting). So I personally was chomping at the bits. Fudge the weather, we can handle it. How could we call ourselves British if we let rain ruin our holiday!

Out of the campsite we rode down the hill...well up one hill, down another hill, up and down again...into Arnhem. Actually now that I remember, we weren't together. Dave still had to buy a cycle helmet from in town, and I wanted to buy swim-shorts after discovering the europarcs had a mini swimming pool. So we split off to source our separate clothing needs.

Swimming is very nostalgic for me. Well more "messing about" in swimming pools than actual swimming. E.g.: making waves, plonking my fists around, doing underwater challenges and acrobatics. Summer was the best, when the outdoor diving boards and rapids were open. All the fun parts and none of the pounding lengths until your muscles scream and your nose and stomach are filled with chlorine because breathing is hard. Back when I was a small kid swimming lessons would literally end up with me consuming so much chlorine water I would eventually vomit over the side of the pool. Go back to swimming. Vomit some more. Swim. Vomit. Doubt I was popular with lifeguards. I wonder if this early childhood exposure to mass vomiting formed part of the reason why I failed at drinking responsibly for so many years, seemingly very blase about throwing up in random places.

Being in the pool reminds me of a friend I had growing up, we'd hang out whenever he came down to visit his Granny in Faversham. A typical day was a morning swimming pool trip. Then absolutely fiending Heroes of Might and Magic III on PC until our eyes bled. We would stop for some Honey sandwiches, maybe a chocolate nutrigrain bar (still the saddest food product "retirement" of my life. One day the shops had them. The next day they didn't. I would give anything to bring them back). Then we'd be straight back at it 'til it was my pickup time. Fudge I loved that game, what a belter of a soundtrack. I still listen to the soundtrack now and again to reminisce. Oh, the friend was cool too…but not as cool as HoMMIII.

I found a pair of green, flowery shorts in the shop at a neighbouring campsite and went to find the guys. We met up again at a bakery in Arnhem. Why do European people insist on serving boiling hot cups of tea in literal glasses? How am I meant to touch this without burning my hand? Are you braindead? Maybe nobody drinks tea there □. Although I love the way they give you a little biscuit with a drink. Seen some UK places start to do that. Hope it catches on more, despite brexit (**editor note**: What does brexit have to do with this? Are you just trying to sound like you understand or know politics? You only found out the

Queen died and we now have a King last week?). Anyway, after teas and some quick breakfast we're off, Germany-bound. Schnell!

At least the route between Arnhem and Germany is pannenkoeken-flat. Still a tough one on these bikes (for the guys that is. I feel uncomfortable Biggie-smalls'ing myself up.... but c'mon. I'd just done a 250 mile-r. I'm not going to struggle doing under 100km), but I am not concerned about that. What I am concerned about:

The dark clouds loom scarily in the distance as we exit Arnhem. I am a ball of anxiety. I always feel responsible for the happiness of the other people I'm with. Especially when I'm already feeling bad for conning them into riding poop bikes. Maybe it is me being a nice person. Maybe it's also insecurity thinking: Will they still want to be friends with me when we have a miserable day getting absolutely drenched? I'm very glad that after checking the forecast, Dave and Christian both had a cavalier attitude to it, still wanted to do a big ride. As opposed to sitting glumly in the wooden hut being down in the dumps...but are they really prepared for this? Are they mentally ready for riding through an absolute deluge? And will it sour their mood for the rest of cycling on the trip? We reach the tiny village of Loo so of course I have to stop and take a selfie. Dave and Christain don't seem to understand why it's amusing. At least not on the level I do.

Right after this the heavens open up. Dave and Christian put on raincoats and waterproof trousers. I put on my raincoat, but it gets too hot because it's still the middle of summer and over twenty degrees, so off it comes again. On off. On off.

There's Kangaroos in Loo. Yeah. You read that right: Kangaroos. I was up ahead as the guys had stopped faffing with clothing, and I preferred cycling slowly to sitting in the rain. And on my left…on the outskirts of Loo there was a farmhouse, and some fences with what you assume are sheep….but then why do these sheep have pouches? Strange. One of the Kangaroos is albino. Very strange. I cannot get any photos because my phone-screen is cracked and would almost certainly break getting it out in this weather.

The thunder clatters in the distance. I'm actually genuinely scared. Not usually scared by thunder, but we're cycling through remote, submerged farmland. The road is raised up on a wide dyke to avoid it being flooded. So the highest point for miles around is…us! The bikes have rubber tyres, so it shouldn't be "too bad" if we get hit by lightning. But I'm confident enough in my understanding of electricity to be keen to put that theory to the test. Whilst not electrocuted, we're still soaked through. Even waterproof clothing has its limits, and these are being found. Little talking going, it feels very much like a: "let's just get through this" mode. It has to end at some point. We route off of the main dyke-road and onto a smaller cycle path through some lovely fields with tall wildflowers, a lot of purple stuff. Still pissing it down though. Eventually when we cross a bridge over a tributary, we see a house, or just a random building with a lean-to. Whatever it is, it is some cover. Dave wants to stop as his knee is hurting. Who's laughing about saddle-height now? Not even me because I'm wet and grumpy. Everyone is happy to be out of the rain for a bit. We decide we can't stay all day and eventually get going again. As we're leaving the rain gradually diminuendos until it actually stops. Being a hot summer day we dry up pretty fast whilst cycling. The mood and tension eases, and it's a fun cycle the rest of the way. We're spotting signs for German towns, German number-plates (gimme that D baby!), anything to indicate we might be nearly there. There's no border. Just suddenly we see some signs in German, and guess we must have already crossed the border. Christian seems a bit disappointed by this, but I'd experience the same on my Berlin trip. One minute you're in one European country, and all of sudden you're in another. No fanfare.

The perfect cyclepath in the Netherlands turns to dodgy paving and bricks. That's another way to tell you've left the Netherlands and entered Germany. We reached Emmerich around lunchtime. The only bakery there was a massive disappointment, to me at least. I knew what the Germans were capable of. And it was significantly more than this. I'd been hyping them up so much….and this was just so lacklustre. Felt slightly embarrassed and kept having to reiterate this is not what I thought was amazing. Like when you go to show someone what you remembered as a really funny vid…but it's nowhere near as funny as you remember, and oh god they're not laughing. And it goes on for 30 more seconds. And there's just tense silence. And you're both embarrassed. How did a short video cause so much awkwardness. Ground swallow me up! Oh well. Anyway, we had a nice lunch sat outside on the Rhine. Well, at a cafe looking at the Rhine. We weren't on a boat.

Picked up some supplies from a small shop and it was back the way we came. Maybe it was the long lunch break, but the struggling began before we were even back in the Netherlands. Our pace slowed a lot. Dave with his dodgy knee, and Christian hanging off the back, doing bursts of energy, then crawling. But we had to just keep pushing to get home. So we pushed…just very slowly. Veeerrry. Slllloooowwwwwwly. Grannies were blasting past us with their weekly shopping in their basket. A little girl on rollerblades zipped by us. I'm not joking, I think the second half of the day may have been at a whopping 8.5mph average.

The German excursion became the biggest riding day for Dave and Christian. They didn't say it, but I think they were not keen to be so far away from home with nothing left in the tank again. We had some chill days instead, combining cycling and train. The next day we rode to and from Ede through the woods, taking the train the rest of the way to Utrecht. We chilled at the botanical garden in Utrecht: Butterflies love cycling tops. Went to a nice micro-brewery. After a couple of pints we rode like absolute baboons. Utrecht is super busy with cyclists and we nearly had a big crash when I crossed not thinking about whether Dave and Christain would also have enough time to cross. They did not. Christian had to panic-brake and essentially fall off his bike to avoid a t-bone with a flat-out road cyclist zooming by.

After Utrecht Dave and Christian decided to have a rest-day on the other day with shite weather forecast. I was secretly very excited. This was a chance for me to test my legs on this monstrosity of a bike. Cycling with slower friends is chill and fun. But simultaneously, after a while your legs are just chomping at the bit: "*Release me! Set me free!*". So today I released them. Canterbury Bicycling Club has a yearly challenge, where you have to do at least one big ride every month. To get the Platinum level, you must do a 200km ride every month. Even in deep winter. 100 miles would be Gold, 75 miles silver, 50 bronze . I was on for Platinum still. But it was nearing the end of the month, and I'd forgotten to get the 200km done. This was going to be the last weekend, so either I did it on this rest-day for Christian and Dave...or I'd have to take a day off from work next week. Or I would just fall down to the Gold category, but that was never going to be an option (**editor note**: I'm editing this on 30th November. The day before completing the yearly platinum challenge! ☐)

So I plotted a massive triangle. The first bit going back down South, deeper into Germany, determined to find a "worthy" bakery. I had to prove to the guys I wasn't bullshitting about the bakeries. Maybe I could bring them back something to convince them. Then it headed West, all the way to the town of Vegel. I wanted to see if I would recognise it from Band of Brothers...(**editor note**: turns out I'd misremembered the town in episode 4, it was actually Neunen, not Vegel, but I didn't know that until I got back. Easy company did travel through Vegel, but the major battle was at Neunen. But on the positive side, Vegel had a lovely big church, with a great frozen yoghurt place next to it. Doubt Neunen would have been as nice. So I can't complain). And then just completing the triangle coming back from Vegel to Arnhem.

The first bakery I went to after crossing the Rhine was underwhelming. So I went even further. Passed a place called Wunderland Kalkar...which might be a theme-park? But on that cloudy summer morning, it looked like a concrete monstrosity and seemed hilarious that Germans would consider this Soviet-bloc looking place as a "Wunderland".

The second bakery was a lot better. No bienenstich, but a great doughnut and some top pastries. None made it back to the guys. Probably not quite worth the trek, but I needed to do 200km, so why not. And it livens up these long rides to have some "sidequests". It rained off and on. But now that I was now free to smash it, I stayed warm and the rain felt refreshing. Also the massive coffee at the bakery helped. I'm sure I've said this before, but my avoidance of caffeine on regular days means it hits like crystal meth when it comes. I physically change when I feel it kicking in. Narrow my shoulders and elbows. Head forwards. Shoulder blades back. Like a leopard stalking its kill. I become predator. The road my prey. I feed off the insanity of bombing it along in repugnant weather on such a ludicrous bike. It has been a slow and gentle start to the day. But now I was eating the miles and might be back well before dark.

I am listening to a lot of Kneecap, Irish rap, and Fontaines DC new album, Irish rock. Also got back into Fight Like Apes, Irish indie-pop. Seem to be listening to everything Irish at the moment. No major calamities on this ride, the bike holds up well, it's tiring but good tiring. Hit some big forest hills in Oosterbeek just outside Arnhem. Stopped for dinner there after struggling up the last big hill. Ordered a fancy risotto, feeling very out of place in my sweaty cycling gear. But didn't care. I'd earnt this risotto. Always feel more at ease around Dutch people. Don't know why, just do. Funnily enough Christian and Dave had been in Oosterbeek on their rest day as well, at the airborne museum. Didn't bump into them though. Finished the ride of climbing out of Arnhem back up to the campsite. 200km ride done. Nice one me :)

The final cycling day was another chill group cycle. Into Nijmegen and back. Along cycle routes following typical Dutch canals. A cool cycling museum in Nijmegen, and a pretty town centre with literal mini-streams flowing down the main street. Views of the big bridges over the Waal river. Overall a nice holiday filled with beer and pancakes.

Completely against the spirit of this book! Though I had been ruminating on Gary again on this trip.

Interlude 3: Random Shit and Non-Cycling Life Updates

After the Berlin trip, the Gary situation was left a bit cliffhangery. I'd tried to keep it very casual, "*Hey are you around on friday to do something?*", so the "*No, I'm busy that day*" didn't fully clarify if there was nothing there. Roles reversed, if I was mega-keen on the other person, I'd have said "No, but I'm free blah…". So I had very low expectations, below 10%...but you don't know how other people will interpret things and respond. So it was intensely frustrating for me not being 100% sure. Wondering if I was going to miss out on a wonderful woman, just because we were both a little dense, and I was too pussy to make it 100%. It was the kind of thing where I knew if I never explicitly asked, I would regret it, and it could bug me for the rest of my life.

When I am nervous, it feels like a portal opens up in the back of my mouth. Which random sentences fly out of, and straight into the world...having at no point resided inside my brain. The kind of sentences that raise your own eyebrows as they come out. Where you wish you could just admit:

"*Look ignore what I just said. I don't actually think or believe any of that. I think I just have demons in my mouth. Don't listen to them.*". But that sounds even weirder, so you're just stuck in a whirlpool of weirdness.

So I was bricking it a bit, and it would be shite if I said something weird enough to make it...well weird...between us. So I crafted a rough speech, the vague idea of my points, with a couple of scripted jokes made to sound off-the-cuff (like all good standups).

When you want or need to talk to someone alone, it's maddening how difficult it can be to find time with them alone, without making it odd. "*Hello, would you like to come down to the basement with me...alone. I have something I need to ask you? Why are you running? The basement is the other way*". I guess you could lie. But I'm a terrible fibber.

Anyway, it finally came at some point, everyone splitting off, and only she was heading off to a tube station in the same direction as me. I'd had two whole half-pints* and was buzzing.

*The half-pint manifesto

(Or the 284.131 millilitre manifesto for the Europeans) EU

- Half-pints are a fundamentally superior drinking experience versus whole pints.
- Nowadays they are literally 0.5x the price of a pint (nearly everywhere) so you're not losing money on them
- Lower average drink temperature
- Allows you to try and sample a wider variety of drinks
    - and if one is pish....you've only got half as much to struggle through
    - e.g. I know several people who have got a pint of sour beer for the first ever time...then spent the next 40 minutes sipping and crinkling up their face. If you'd have halved it, you'd have halved the misery.
- Some pubs serve you halves in a pint cup, and seem to actually give you closer to 2/3rd pint
    - note: This may just be bar-people seeing my dishevelled freezer-bag-wallet* and taking pity.
    - *That's a different manifesto for a different day.
- Leads you to drink more responsibly

- Oh wow, I've had 4 drinks. I'm proper on it! Better slow down before I get too wrecked. When really it's only 2 pints!
- Zero bus-shelter sleeping nights since committing to the half-pint philosophy.
- Every time I buy a drink and the machine shows over £5, a little part of me dies inside
- Fewer toilet trips
  - Could be a con if you love toilets
- More trips to the bar is not necessarily bad. Nice to stretch your legs. Get those 10,000 steps in.

I will agree that above some threshold, bar-queuing time becomes the limiting factor, trumping all listed positives. However if there's no queue, half-pints all the way my friend!

Fuck this was hard. Riding 250 miles in a day is a walk in the cake compared to explaining your feelings to someone. I was trying to pick up the courage whilst walking with her. The first part suddenly stumbled out of my mouth, and by that point it felt committed. It was easier to continue with the points I'd considered, than try and back-pedal. Apart from a several second pause followed by "*I've forgotten how to do words*" as my brain just thought: "*fuck. I'm actually doing this. I didn't expect to actually be doing this.*", apart from that it was going well. Well, going well in the sense that I was getting it out. I have a habit of avoiding eye-contact when I'm concentrating hard. Not deliberately, it's not even really avoiding. It's more just I'm concentrating on the words so much my eyes stop working. They could be looking anywhere. They're still background-processing, scanning the horizon for threats and terrorists that I may need to disable. But I don't really "see" anything with them. I interpret other people through tone of voice anyway, and the micro-sounds listening people give in conversations, so vision usually isn't super important. Her voice felt tense, not superbad tense, but like cogs whirring in brain. But certainly not jubilant. So I could sense how it was going to play out, but at this stage I might as well commit to it.

And yeah, there was a good reason why we should just stay friends. I'm not going to put it here, because unsurprisingly I quite like the person, and I don't want to violate their privacy, in-case anybody reading can clock who they are. I got some genuine laughs out of the semi-scripted jokes so I'm glad it wasn't just a terribly embarrassing ordeal.

Weird situation. When you've just been dealt, well dealt yourself, an emotional hammer blow...but at the same time, you're so God damn proud of yourself that you also can't help beaming from ear to ear.

Now to move on from this soppy emotional bullshit, and back to bludgeoning my body with bicycles.

There was the first cyclocross race of the year in early September. It's not really worthy of its own chapter. It went shite.

For those not in the know, cyclocross is taking road bikes, putting off-road tyres on them, and racing them around grassy fields. Although being a winter only sport, that grass turns into mud within minutes. So there's lots of slipping. Lots of sliding. Lots of crashing. It's really fun being able to push your bike to the limit of crashing, without it being a disaster if you actually do crash. Often it gets so muddy you have to get off your bike and run with it in sections. Such a silly sport. There's literally official rules saying your tyres can't be wider than 33mm, otherwise they're "too grippy" and it's cheating! xD

The September event is usually the odd one out. Early enough in the year that it's not an actual mudfest, and is usually very dry and dusty. Tyre choice in cyclocross is similar to Formula 1. If you go out on a dry track in wets, you're super slow. Or a wet track in slicks, you'll be spinning more than Torvill and Dean. So you want tyres for every scenario, but tyres are also kind of expensive. With only 1 dry race a year, I'd never bothered investing in a set of dryies. But this year I felt that this could be my best round of the season, so I splunged on a front and rear dryie. Our summer had been a pile of rainy shite, but late August and the start of September we were finally getting the sun we so deserved. So without hesitation I put the dryies on the bike the week of the race.

The day before the race, the weather forecast I saw claimed "sporadic, light showers". I should have taken this as a warning to at least be prepared for a last-minute change to mud tyres. But I had invested so much into prepping for a dry-race, I was tunnel-visioned.

Aaaaand it pissed it down. More rain in a day than we'd had for weeks. Oh dear. The course is at a local school, around the playing fields, we even ride through the long jump pit. I spent most of the pre-race phase hiding under a tenty thing in the school carpark. When I turned up on the grid, I glanced at all the other riders. Everyone had bigger knobs than me. Everyone. On a slippy course with so many tight turns, my pathetic knobs were not gonna cut the mu(d)stard. Terrible pun, for terrible tyres xD.

Due to results last year, I was on the front row....somewhere I did not deserve to be. So at the start several people immediately whooshed past me. Even more after the first corner. Being the first race of the season I hadn't got into "racing mode", where I can just tell myself: "Everyone else can go flip themselves. I'm gonna do whatever it takes to get the best result for me". So without this competitive mindset, I took wide, sweeping lines into corners. It let the faster people bomb past me, avoiding holding them up and ruining their race. But when I glanced around at the end of the lap....no-one was behind me. Oh.

Bloody hell, even the people who do local cyclocross train and race hard for it. It's the complete opposite of all the rides I'd done all summer. Rather than a whole day of pacing yourself, this is just batter your body into the ground for an hour, as close to max heart-rate as you can stay without dying.

The dry tyres were no bueno. Every corner the bike would try to wriggle out from under me. Post-race I had massive blisters on each 2nd finger, both from where I'd had to constantly "catch" slides and hold the bike upright with so much force. Proud that I only had one actual crash, some last-lap madness. Where your brain stops working under the intense physical effort. I was losing so much time in corners, when one of the leaders lapped me I thought: "*I'll watch him through the next corner and do the exact same thing*".....Instantly on the ground, no time to catch this slide. Don't know what I was thinking.

My body adjusted after the first two laps, and I was able to make up a few places, coming home in a respectable enough 21st. Followed by a long 90 minute ride home through the pouring rain, made even longer by a puncture which took ages to fix, as everything was slimy with mud.

King of the Boughton ~~Hill~~ Mountain

I think I've slightly fucked up the sequencing. Pretty sure this happened at the end of August, and the CX was on the first weekend of September, but do you really care?

There's this thing in cycling (and running as well) called an "Everesting". It's a personal challenge where you cycle (or run) up and down the exact same hill. Time after time, until you've officially reached the height of Mount Everest.

Mount Everest is pretty tall, nearly 9000 metres, or 30000 feet. That's a lot of up. I'd learnt about it the year before, and like any big challenge, the "I wonder if I could achieve that" would just sporadically pop into my head. I went for a half-hearted attempt last year up Soleshill, local to me. Gave up half-way through, swearing: "only an actual psychopath could finish one of these".

I'd had ideas of trying it earlier in the year, but went for the Berlin challenge and the 250-mile chase the Sun instead. Thinking I'll save other challenges for future years. But as the year drew on, maybe I was just jaded and suffering overtraining fatigue, but I was telling myself that next year I was going to cut down on the cycling. When you're lying to your friends and family about how much you do, you might have a bit of a problem. And it's not just the roughly 20 hours of cycling a week to prepare for long-distance stuff. It's also all the bike maintenance that comes with it. Then spending so much time eating enough calories to fuel that. Then so much time on the toilet expelling half that food. It just wasn't leaving room for anything besides work, sleep and cycling.

Maybe if my work was more creatively fulfilling I'd be happy with just work, sleep, cycle. But let's face facts. It's not. So I will occasionally dabble with new musical instruments or other projects. But I'd end up focussing on cycling and bin them. This year I'd started writing, like proper writing. A fiction book, a "novel". The hook and part of story is around how easy it is to smuggle drugs into the UK by bicycle. The book was...is?...going to be 50% breaking bad on bicycles. Then 50% watership down (but with mice...I have a pair of field mice that live in the shed at the bottom of my garden. And half the story would be from their perspective, in the narrator's shed.). So the working title, pending legal battles, is "Of Men and Mice"!

It was going surprisingly well. People were saying it was very reminiscent of "Notes from the Underground" by Dostoevsky. People being me. Because fuck letting other people read and critique it when it's 89% your life. Also "Notes from the Underground" is not one of his highly rated works, but it's my favourite. Although I've never actually even finished "War and Peas" or "The Brothers Kalashnikov". A less ponse-y way to describe the books feel would be "Peep Show". I mean it was going well. I've now left it untouched for the past 2 months so it may never happen (**editor note**: 4 months, close to 5 now xD), but back around end of August I was still full of enthusiasm, and thinking I wouldn't have much time to cycle in 2025, because I'd be so busy being a successful bestselling author and all-round delusional guy.

So I'm not expecting to have as much time for ultra-distance cycling next year. Plus I'm now up to 85kg (**editor note**: below 82kg now, being a vegan who is not allowed to eat anything tasty ☐), despite being under 6 foot, and it just seems to keep heading in one direction. So if we combine these two factors, this could be the highest power-to-weight ratio I ever have. So is this going to be my last year where doing an everest is realistically achievable?

Note: It probably seems a bit obscene me writing about these massive cycles, where strava claims I burn several thousand calories a day...yet still I put on weight? Well I actually find these megarides detrimental. For starters, to finish the megaride, you need to eat close-ish to what you burn anyway. And then in the days afterwards, your cravings for high fat, high sugar food are super intense. Trading your firstborn levels of intense. I don't want to say "I always fail to resist the cravings" as that's thinking negatively about the future. But **so far** I have never managed to resist. So the dirty eating after the big ride builds bad habits. By the time you've got your eating back on track...you're calorie positive overall.

I do think cyclists tend to be a little too weight obsessed, and for most people eating more, rather than less, will make them faster with higher power. At least in the UK where we have hills rather than mountains....but that means eating lots of proper food. Rather than junk food like I stray towards. The local rider who has impressed me the most with fitness improvements, Johnny, but big Johnny, tall not wide; he did it through just getting up every morning at 6am, and bashing out about 90 minutes each day, at relatively relaxed pace (zone 2). Maybe one or two higher intensity sessions a week max. Almost everyone trying to burn "excess" fat tries to be cheeky, go too hard, fly too close to the sun...and it blows up in their...my...faces. The consistent, steady work is what really gets results. Anyway enough lecturing from someone who can't keep a box of high-fibre cereal in the house without eating it all in one sitting...then groaning on the toilet for forty minutes as he births a Guinness record breaking turd and wonders "Is this a bit what it's like to have a baby?"....on with the story.

Realising it could be now or never, one day I spur of the moment just decided...fuck it. This Saturday, I'm giving it a go.

It would be a different hill this time. Boughton hill. Everesting is not for the faint of heart. You do need to be quite a good (amateur) cyclist to do it. I only know one local cyclist who has managed it. Dave Carter. He's a weirdo in the best sense, I mean that as a genuine compliment. Part of what has attracted me so much to cycling, is the serious amateurs do tend to be a bit unhinged and proper characters. He also did it up Boughton hill and said that was the only sensible hill in our area to go for. He's kind of right. There's other hills which are technically possible, but would be even harder due to weird gradient changes. Or the downhills are gravelly and way too sketchy when your brain is done-zo. A couple of years earlier Dave, Nick and Colin attempted it for charity, on an incredibly hot day. Dehydration got the best of most of them. Only Dave finished it, on his own, late at night (possibly another local cyclist, Owen had come out to cheer him on...but the other failed cyclists had trudged off home in disgrace).

My alarm went off at 4:30am on the Saturday. I pulled on my gear. Filled my pockets with sandwiches and snacks. Filled my backpack with even more. Out the door and off. Boughton hill is just a 20 minute ride from me. I pulled up at the top, dawn just about breaking, and chucked my backpack into a bush near the top of the hill. At the top is a horse stable on the right, and a cul-de-sac on the left where I can safely do a 180. Then down is pretty much a dead-straight line. You can't see the bottom from the top because it levels out slightly before it. But after going over the lip you can see all the way down into the village. The hill is just over 190-feet, average gradient about 7%. Meaning I would need to do 153 ascents, each one taking between 4 and 5 minutes...definitely stretching to longer towards the end.

The downhill part is great fun at the start, whizzing over 40mph. At the bottom there is a left turning and a right turning on either side, making it slightly sketchy with cars pulling out, but at least it is good visibility. Each time I reached the bottom, I would brake and use the right hand turn to 180 and go back up for another ascent.

It went fairly smoothly at the start. To chill myself out and not get carried away I was listening to relaxing music: Tycho, Washed Out, Daywave, The Drums. I was trying to keep my heart-rate below 150, which I sort of achieved, but definitely kept it below 160. Even trying to go as slow as you can....it's hard to go as slow as you should. And I'd pay for sitting at 149 heart-rate later…

Everesting is the most fucking boring thing in the world. It is not really comparable to other long distance cycling challenges. Other long distance challenges you are going somewhere, you have a goal, you see new sights to keep your brain entertained. But up and down. Up and down. Up and down. I feel like whoever wrote the myth of sisyphus, never actually spent a day rolling a boulder up and down a hill. If he'd actually have done that, rather than spending his days chain-smoking and drinking coffees in petite french cafes....then we'd have gotten a very different book. Although I am a major Camus fan. I appreciate his "philosophy" can be read as a normal novel. They are actual stories you can enjoy in their own right. Therefore you get to choose how much you interact and think about the ideas behind it. Not like Sartre, who just thrusts his existentialism straight in your face. If Sartre was alive today, he'd definitely be the kind of guy to send unsolicited dick pics; for sure. Camus is clearly the classier of the two. But maybe he should try an everesting before dispensing wisdom on a meaningful life.

But yeah, it's mind-numbing. You also don't want to focus too much on how much you've done, because 15 reps of this hill is a lot. And it puts in perspective the rest of the challenge ahead. Ah I try not to use the phrase hill-reps anymore when training. "Rep" is a very aggressive sounding word, makes training feel very daunting. I prefer the to say "15 Hilly-Willies". "Reps" sounds like you're doing super hardcore training, "hilly-willies" sounds you're just joking around and having a laugh. Easier to motivate yourself to do some "Hilly-Willies"....anyway, yeah at 15 the hill is already taking it's toll....but you haven't even done 10% yet. You've got at least 135 left. If you focus on the numbers, this feels impossible. Pro athletes do "chunking" where they chunk a big challenge into reasonable sub-goals. But maybe most pro athletes are dumb...but my brain just extrapolates and I can't hide from it that I've got

135 more. So I have to go just one at a time. Maybe that's still chunking.

Dave said that when he did it, for him, in a way it wasn't that much of a challenge, because in his head...once he's started doing something and told himself he's going to do it...it's unthinkable to give up. It's already done. But for me, it was very thinkable. Very, very thinkable. I'd already failed it last year. My form had been dropping since the 250 miler and I hadn't been out much. The prominent driving force for me was: "If I fail...I'm probably going to have to go through all the pain and bullshit again next year". And I never want to try this again.

The local Canterbury Bicycle Club ride was heading near to Boughton around 11am, so a lot of them diverted off and did one ascent with me. This was around the 40-ish mark? Seeing everyone and their enthusiasm was a great boon and gave me the boost to push through the "fuck, I'm not even that near halfway" section.

There's not much to really describe about the rest of it, other than the odd person turning up. I just went up and down the hill. Pete turned up around rep 70 to say hi. By this point I was really struggling. I'd taken a caffeine drink and some supergels (2-to-1 ratio of glucose to fructose giving you the fastest absorption of sugar possible). But these were to be saved for the final push near the end, to carry me over the line. However I was so fucked by the 70's, and the sun and heat were getting to me (it was mid-20's), that I thought....either I'm having these last-resort resources now...or I'm packing up and going home. So I might as well have them now, and see what happens at the end. This was probably the worst time mentally. On the downhills I remember looking down at my computer, seeing 43mph and thinking: "If one of these cars blindly pulls out of the junction and t-bones me...I think I'd be pretty OK with that." I was not prepared to give up. But also I just really, really wanted it to be over. By any means.

Near to 100 I was close to...not death. But failure. Which seems as bad as death at times. I hadn't had any breaks at all early on. Just preferring to ride slow and steadily, at least what I thought was steadily. At around 3pm I pulled off to do my "pit-stop", take fresh snacks out of my stashed rucksack, and refill water bottles...but I just collapsed onto the ground. Just laid there in semi-foetal position for I'm not sure how long. Maybe 5 minutes. Maybe 15? I eventually forced myself up and cranked out another few reps. Josh turned up, a local mountain bike and cyclocross racer who I ride with a bit (often gives me very handy lifts to races due to my car-less situation). He'd brought a couple of spare gels with him, which I gratefully took. This was probably around 5pm, maybe 110 in or so? It wasn't just me that was struggling. The bike was now making a "Raarch...raarch...rarch" horrible noise with each pedal revolution up the hill. Seems like my bottom bracket was done for. I had no choice other than to keep going really. If the bike fully broke I'd have another excuse to stop. I stomped on the pedals harder.

Nick, the cyclist who attempted it before and got stymied by dehydration, turned up with his van full of snacks at about 130. I had another break here, and devoured crisps, pancakes, sausage-roll type things. Anything and everything

If it wasn't for Josh and Nick dropping off food near the end, and also my sister dropping off spare lucozade around midday...I don't think I could have finished. But after people have taken time out of their day and helped you, you feel like you can't let them down by giving up. When I said goodbye to Nick I was optimistic saying: "*Nah, I don't need anymore food. I've only got about 30 left to do*". Turns out 30 is a lot. May have been fairly delusional.

But once you've got over 80% it's hard to fail so close to finish. So with the "rarch....rarch" sound getting louder. The roads getting quieter and calmer. The sun setting. I reached around 142 in the darkness, around 10pm. The last 10 didn't feel easy....but at this point you could walk up and down the remainder. I actually couldn't remember how tall Everest was by this point. So I just kept going until I hit 30,000 feet on my computer. 153 reps in total. Started at around 5am. Ended after 11pm. I sat down and watched the stars for a bit. A beautifully clear night. I hadn't realised it, but also the start of a "meteor window". Pretty cool seeing one big one whoosh over after my big ordeal. Felt fitting. I gathered up my rucksack and soft-pedalled home. Shame I immediately passed two squished hedgehogs just past the top of the hill, which kind of knocked my mood down. But whatever. It was done. And I never have to attempt it again. Some people try double-everesting, or the Marianas trench challenge. But eff that. I am done. I'm out. Good luck to anyone psychotic enough to do even more, but I can't. Maybe it'll be like squeezing out children, where over time you forget the horror, go in for round two, and end up wondering....how have I got myself in this position again? But for now the memory is still a little too fresh.

183.84 mi   **17:24:27**   **30,164** ft   814

Distance   Moving Time   Elevation   Historic Relative
                                                    Effort

140 w   **8,763** kJ

Estimated Avg   Energy Output
Power

	Avg	Max	
			Show Less
Speed	10.6 mi/h	47.8 mi/h	
Heart Rate	132 bpm	166 bpm	
Calories	9,415		
Temperature	21 °C		
Elapsed Time	18:32:29		

London 2 Paris Chapter 1: The Fellowship of the Ri(di)ng (Bicycles)

The next adventure was another one with company. Our company, Generic Finance Company: Business to Business Something Something. It has a London and a Paris office...so a few of the Londonites, decided it would be a cool challenge to attempt a London → Paris cycle. Canterbury is only an hour train away from London, so I got myself up there the night before for the monthly company piss-up, and dragged myself, semi-rotting, to the office for our 8am start.

There was a mix of experiences. At one end: Daniel, who should have been coming, super competent. He does so much crit racing in London. I feel like he told me maybe 40 or 50 races a year? That sounds mental for someone like me who's local cyclocross racing season is once a month for 5 months. He's properly sponsored and everything. Gets free wheels, free gear; jealous. Maybe if I was good-looking enough to be in a Bikmo advertisement I'd get free shit as well. Then at the other end, the deep end, for him at least: Martin. He has technically ridden a bike before. But following behind him you wouldn't know it. Borrowing a friend's bike to commute to the London office for the week before the trip, he'd already been involved in a London traffic pileup. But he was active and young. So despite being the least likely to make it to Paris, so long as he stayed on two wheels, easier said than done, he could and should do it.

The Cast:

Tim – How can I say he sounds a bit posh but in a nice way? Not even that posh, can just say words properly. Not a geezer. Spikey hair. Soon-to-be-dad energy.

Elena – Spanish. Jet black hair. On a brand new Van Rysel and getting used to fancy road pedals. Bold choice switching from flat pedals for this trip

Martin – Also jet black hair. East Asian British. Lightweight. Renting a road bike for the challenge.

Ollie – Can't remember if he has hair. If so, it must be short. Probably the most athletic and muscley out of the non-Johnnies. A bit overqualified for this challenge.

Johnny – Flowing curly locks down to the shoulders. Hint of a beard. Thunderful thighs. Ass of the gods. Proper beefcake. (editor note: I don't care if these visual descriptions are unbalanced. It's my fucking book. If they want to have superlatives thrown at their feet they can write their own fudging books. Capiche!)

Daniel :..... X :(

Day 1 got off to an auspicious start. Daniel had already "Boromir"'d himself, way too early for this metaphor to work. The doctor had informed Daniel, our most veteran cyclist, that trying to cycle to Paris would almost definitely cause his leg to explode. So he was out.

Without his savoir faire; we had nobody who knew which specific sunglasses and rapha tops looked the coolest. Potential disaster. This could have severely impacted our street cred. But Ollie had saved the day, sorting us out with some incredibly snazzy Generic Finance Company cycling tops.

So we looked pretty fly in our pre-ride photo op in front of a gherkin. Thanks to friend turned photographer Alex for arriving precisely 15 minutes later than our hard deadline...but somehow exactly when we planned to leave. Those 15 minutes surely wouldn't matter? Or would they? ....No they wouldn't. But they nearly did.

The sun was shining, yet it was flipping freezing. The UK having expired its allotted 3 weeks of summer weather. Hands were cold, but everyone was too buzzing from the excitement of getting underway to stop and apply gloves. It was nice to be around the excited aura of many peoples first big cycling challenge.

The parkour for day 1 was very hilly. Over 4000ft total (That's over 4000 Meatball Marinara footlong subs from Subway ®). Daniel had sensibly suggested a flatter route. But with him out of the picture, Johnny was free to take over as route-master and properly emphasise the brutality of the challenge. The whole group absolutely smashed the first big hill up to Crystal Palace. Same for all the hills around London. Tim had graciously offered to carry a lot of Martin's gear in his two large rear paninis. Martin repaid this by zooming past him up the early hills. Such great progress from everyone erased all doubts around "athletic ability". It made it seem like the "challenge" may not pose much of a challenge at all. It would be a "leisurely stroll" to Paris. But, this was leading to a false sense of security. The cost of all this hill smashing was rapidly depleting glycogen stores.

Before the ride, someone confessed to me:
"*Im concerned about Martin*".
I had responded with
"*The only thing I'm concerned about is your lack of faith. Martin is young. He plays football. Martin will be absolutely fine!*"

Martin was not fine....

Well technically Martin was completely fine......up until the point he was suddenly not fine.

The fast early pace would eventually lead to many struggling. However Martin was the only one whose sugar-deprived brain led him dirt-tracking. The woods were calling him. He answered. And without the sufficient bike-handling skills to support such off-road excursions, there was only one outcome. From ahead all that could be heard was a skrrr of wheels on stones and dirt. Then the crunch.

Thankfully Martin and the bike were technically OK. Banged up and scratched to fuck, but OK to ride. Or so it seemed. 20 minutes later, coming down a big hill, I hear Martin's bike making a very loud and dodgy clunking sound. We stop and I inspect. One of the front spokes is completely broken and is flailing everywhere. There's no other option. The flailing spoke must be amputated. It pulls out fine, and then I go to loosen…or tighten…the spokes either side, which should True the wheel even sans-spoke. For some Godforsaken reason the spokes are a strange archaic width, and my 3-different-width spoke tool can't handle the job. The wheel was so buckled, it bashed into the brake pads and was unridable. Even worse, it was nearly lunchtime. Tim, Elena and Ollie were up the road. Johnny was silently, internally, absolutely losing his shit. Mainly because phone calls to the others were focusing slightly too much on "the lunch problem", when Martin's bike is completely fucking fucked, in the middle of fucking nowhere!

Tim phoned a conveniently close bike-shop to organise a last minute repair. That's if we could get the bike there. He doubled back and met Johnny and Martin (obviously after delegating the lunchspot scouting and table-saving to Ollie and Elena). After semi-disconnecting the front brakes, and some duck-tape, Martin's bike was """"rideable"""" (according to Tim). Not according to Johnny. So Tim was the one who braved riding it to the shop, whilst Martin took Tim's bike. The 3 stragglers regrouped with Ollie and Elena, in the small town of.

Whilst waiting for the bike to be fixed, we raided the cafe next door for takeaway lunch. Sausage rolls and cakey flapjack type things. It should have been a quick job. Unfortunately the archaic spoke was causing strife for the mechanic as well. Irreplaceable at short notice. The shop, (note to editor: Insert shop name here. Although it can't have been very memorable) In-Gear Cycle Sport (**editor note**: That genuinely took me 20 minutes of map hunting to find where we stopped. How flipping lucky are we that there is a small bike shop tucked away in the tiny Forest Row), offering a whole new wheel for only £40. We took it.

Downside: by the time this was sorted, it was now incredibly tight on making the 5pm Newhaven ferry. And if we missed that, the next one was at 2am. Panic ensued. Some cowards even started googling train times.

But it got fixed and we got moving. We really put the hammer to the metal and opened up the throttle towards Newhaven. Ditching the planned route for a more direct plan, braving the busy main roads to Lewes. The pace and the incessant hills really pushed people to their limits. We had to stop a few times for drinks and food, many people not comfortable doing it on the bike. Although to be fair, when I am gonking, eating and drinking on bike starts to feel a little dangerous, so I often quickly do it at junctions. However only I had special shorts with quickdraw snack access. So stopping it had to be. Each stop ate away the minutes and left especially Tim and I grimacing as we checked the time. But, barring the bungee cables precariously carrying Martin's carrier bag dangling loose and nearly getting tangled in the spokes...we made good time. As we reached the long, single road leading into Newhaven Tim declared we could relax slightly. We couldn't slow down much per se. But we were going to make it.

The road into Newhaven is pretty obnoxious. Narrow and with blind bends. So we accidentally created a massive tailback on the winding road. If we'd have had more time we would have pulled over and let a load through. But I didn't want to tempt fate and a late puncture dash our dreams. The cars were finally freed anyway when we had to stop because Johnny's bag and jeans came loose, spilling an obscene amount of bright-pink birth control all over the road. There is genuinely a very reasonable and sensible explanation for this, which I don't have time to go into. It's also a surprisingly boring reason.

We arrived with multiple minutes to spare. Met Tim's parents who took some photos and chatted a bit. Big cycle fans, Tim's Mum trying to talk about the Vuelta, but the stress of the journey down had left me a bit socially stunted. Not being annoyed by conversation, but just becoming a yes-no merchant.

The 4hr ferry was ridden. Next stop Dieppe. Great views of Seven Sisters. Elena, Tim, Ollie and Martin played a card game. Johnny sat with his head in hands, trying not to groan too loud. He had to spend 2 more days cycling with these cretins. Everyone assumed he suffered from seasickness.

Getting in late, we stayed overnight in Dieppe. Dragging fully-loaded bikes up the narrowest and steepest staircase in France was an interesting end of day challenge. But it was the best 1-star hotel I've ever stayed in.

London 2 Paris Chapter 2: The Return of the (fuc)King (hills!)

Breakfast ☐. It was eaten. To avoid a repeat of day 1, with Martin fully bonking; the rest of us went into helicopter parent mode…aggressively so (fully armed Boeing AH64 Apache gunships). It was borderline force-feeding. Martin our battery Turkey needing to be prepared for Christmas. The incessant badgering may have slightly broken his brain. At the lunch cafe, he ended up stealing several ketchup sachets, using them as energy gels later on.

We were up and off early, leaving by 8AM. This was going to be the big day. We were doing the bulk of the French leg to Paris in one fell swoop. Then we could be in Paris for lunch the following day. Tim had picked another budget-squeezing hotel in Les Mureaux, which was a long trek. But I'm never going to complain about a long cycle. And nobody else batted an eye.

It was a cool crisp morning. Salt n Vinegar maybe. Actually really cool. Cold. Freezing for this time of year. Our fingers white. One by one each of us stopped and gloved up. We followed "Avenue le Vert". The "official nice route" for London -> Paris, set up for the London Olympics. Endless miles of pure cyclepath. The start was flat as a crepé. Spirits were high. With no hard time deadline, people were supremely confident.

Throughout the day we bumped into many other cyclists also attempting London -> Paris. It should have been a bit worrying that these people looked like proper cyclists, yet were attempting a far smaller day 2 than us. Around 11am

Tim made a friend who told us there were hardly any hills en route. The hills kicked in around 11:10am. Some friend. We remembered we'd smashed the early hills day 1, only to end with great suffering towards the finish...so the strategy for day 2 seemed to be...smash the early hills again!??

I'm going to put this down to perfect weather and too much caffeine ☕. Meaning people probably didn't realise how high the pace was (But I have a fancy cycle computer, with lots of metrics, so I can categorically say that "Yes we were repeating day 1. Yes we were digging ourselves into another hole" □□). Elena seemed to be the only person playing the energy conservation game at this early stage, hanging off the back up the climbs and we split apart before regrouping at the tops.

Each hill chipped away at the enthusiasm. Bit by bit. Hill by hill. Early enthusiasm had fully evaporated even before lunch. Avenue le Vert was nice, but not supremely picturesque. And people were getting a bit tired of the twiddly route.
Painfully close to the lunch-town of <forgettable name> (editor note: It was actually Gournay-en-Brey. That's a pretty cool sounding name and not forgettable at all!), Tim punctured.

"*Johnny, you're the expert. You'll be able to sort this out way faster than me*".

20 minutes of faffing later, I finally got the new tube on. It won't inflate. Me and Tim pump furiously for a while, before finally noticing a faint hissing sound. Well well well. I had pinch-punctured the replacement inner-tube. What an expert.

Tim takes over the 2nd fix attempt. This time the tyre is sorted in 3 minutes and we're back rolling. I was secretly quite happy with this puncture. It gave me an excuse to go for it en-route to Gournay-en-Brey, nearly all downhill from this point, and I knew Tim was surprisingly brave and effective at holding the wheel for someone who rarely group-rides.

Elena has chicken again for lunch. Apparently it was better than the ferry chicken she had the night before. I had pizza on the ferry. It was the worst pizza I have ever had. Clearly a frozen one, microwaved for not even long enough to melt the middle cheese. But pizza is like sex. Even bad pizza is still good. After lunch the group, knackered by this point, took a vote on whether to keep following the nice but circuitous "Avenue le Vert". Or take up Tim(li)'s "*We could pass through the Mines!*" offer, which was:

> *Let us trust google maps, it gives a more direct route, potentially shaving off 30 minutes.*

This decision was made similarly to the scene in "Death of Stalin", where nobody in the politburo wants to be on the losing side of a vote. So people comically, edgingly raise and lower their hands. In the end all agreeing to something only one guy really wants.

note:

- A) In truth the group consensus really did want to gamble the shorter route. People were already done-zo and wanted to get the day done and dusted ASAP. I would have preferred avenue vert all the way. But not enough to fight for it, and risk being ostrich sized by the rest of the gang.

- B) If you think "Death of Stalin" is too niche a reference for this write-up; then you can get to fuck! It's a modern classic, and it's been on Netflix for like 7 years! You have no excuse not to have watched it.

Post-lunch:

Anyway, we trusted google maps. And just like Frodo's foolish decision to go for the mines, Google Maps well and truly plundered our nether regions. It would sinisterly attempt to lead us off the road and into the forest at every opportunity. Punishing us with hills when we declined.

Somehow by straying from the original route, we'd managed to turn what could have been 2300ft of climbing, into 4400ft by nightfall. Even more than the first day. And a pretty obscene number for less experienced cyclists. Exhaustion was getting to everyone. Up the steepest hill of the day, steep enough to have literal alpine style hairpins, Tim took a 2mph tumble. This was probably just to try and get us to pity him and forget about his Stalin-esque control and mismanagement of the route-finding. It didn't work. No sympathy for you.

Martin had already gone down in the morning. A patch of mud on the early cycle path out of Dieppe. Elena had a clipless pedal related topple nearer the end. Over half the party had hit the deck at some point. Fortunately Martin and Elena were embarrassed but unscathed. Well Martin was already so scathed, that it was hard to notice if his scathing had gotten stronger. But even before his fall, Tim's knee was breaking down. He was adjusting his saddle to no avail, eventually riding one foot half-off the pedal. Nothing remarkable happened to Ollie. What a boring cunt. ☺

Coming out of a splash-and-dash coffee stop in the town of Gizzors, a grand Gothic Cathedral dominating the skyline and being the focal point of the town, we decidedly ditched

Google Maps. Good riddance. Instead we switched to Strava's "most direct" route-finding. This immediately put us onto a 90kmh road, up an ~8% hill with a blind bend. Nope! Fuck nope! I was in the lead and had pulled to a halt as the cyclepath disappeared and merged into the main road. A quick roundtable indicated nobody seemed keen on the road. And despite Elena and Martin being desperate to just get to our hotel…they had not yet lost the will to live. So we noped the fuck out of that and headed back into Gizzors. We went the scenic way instead. With cycling, and in general....

The scenic route == big fuck-off hills. Not what we needed. But at least the hills wouldn't kill us. Probably wouldn't kill us.⌞OBJ⌝

It really became a slogfest. People were pushed to their absolute limits, past them, and into worlds of fatigue they never dreamed imaginable. Welcome to my crazy world guys. I was genuinely a bit jealous. This was waaaaay beyond the longest rides nearly everyone had done. But nobody complained. Even with the multiple *"oh no, we've changed plan. Now it's a little bit further. Haha"*....No towels were thrown in. You cannot say it was a "jolly" atmosphere. With extreme exhaustion, there's not much talking. Although Elena could be heard muttering to herself. Can't remember if it was "*I can do this!*", or *"I can't do this!"*. Maybe a mix of both. But overall there was a very determined and focused air. We'd made our bed with the optimistic route-planning. Then we'd shit in it. Now we had to just hold our nose and lie in it, just for a few more hours until we reached our booked accommodation.

There was some beautiful scenery and rolling hills. Not entirely sure people were in a fit state to appreciate this, but it was. Johnny appreciated it. Maybe Ollie as well. Hard to tell with Tim. He would be in positive, encouraging dad-mode and put on a brave face, but I could hear him breathing harder than anyone else on my wheel. Some of the downhills were super sketchy, loose gravel that scared even me. Martin maxing out his brakes down some descents. There was one extremely gravelly descent, where literally the whole road was covered. Basically the new, cheap road maintenance strategy we have in the UK. Dump a lorry-load of pebbles on the road, which eventually cars squash down. Tangent: Fecking hate these. They make the roads so sketchy and nearly unrideable for cyclists until they're bedded in. Anyway, there was this super loose stuff across the whole road, down a pretty steep hill. I reached the bottom first and bit my fingers waiting for the others. Everyone turned up except Elena. It had been so long I thought she must have crashed. Just as I started cycling back up the hill, expecting to find her in the gravel, she emerged from round the bend. At about 5mph, looking absolutely terrified. But completely fine. Although she would probably need some new brake-pads shortly after this trip. Luckily we all got through the dodgy descents in one piece.

It flattened out a bit, but still flowing through the countryside. At least the roads were good and potholes weren't too much of a concern. Especially as only I pointed them out, and I'm pretty sure a lot of the gang just tanked each and every one anyway. I did my best Sepp Kuss impression. Sat on the front, and pedalled away at a steady 13mph on the flats. Adjusting it up or down slightly with elevation. We formed a pretty efficient mini-peloton, with Ollie, the only other person not struggling, sweeping from behind. We didn't have many stops. And made them quick when we did. I tried to impart my psychological trick of avoiding looking at how far is left in numbers. Instead focussing on which villages you still have to go through. This stops the road-signs being meaningless gobbledegook, and gets you excited when you see recognisable places e.g. Only 2km until the funnily named town (Wy-dit-Joli-Village). However Tim would consistently shatter that approach, check Google, and declare: "*Only 35km to go chaps*". Not greeted with enthusiasm. Our final destination was Les-Mureax on the Seine, very close to Paris. We were on the South side of it. As we entered from the North, as light was failing, you could feel the relief in the air. I was especially excited for the guys as we were at 98 miles, and this might end up being people's first ever century. I suggested if we ended up just shy, we could do laps around the car park. Again, not greeted with enthusiasm.

We had started at 8am. And it was just gone 8pm, when all 5 of us rolled into the shabby motel. Tim did all the talking. Tim's French is actually very impressive (He has not paid me to say that. He talked the head off the receptionist whilst I chain-drank machine hot chocolates). We'd done 4400ft, and 101 miles total just today alone. Ollie, Elena, Tim and Martin's first imperial century ride □...and potentially the last. At the closest food place we tucked into well deserved crepes (x2 for me. Also the 2nd one I devoured in only 3 mouth-visits. Not sure if everyone else was impressed or aghast. Or even noticed. They seemed surprised that a whole crepe had disappeared in 45 seconds. But I am the pancake-master. Even when I was a child I'd set a 16 pancake record one pancake day before my Granny had to intervene and call it off), pizzas, """"tapas"""" (the Spaniard in the group objected to this spread of onion rings and potatoes being called tapas. A sea of beige), chips and beers. Elena ordered chicken once again.

Then well-earnt sleep. The 2 hard days are over. The final day should be a walk in the cake…

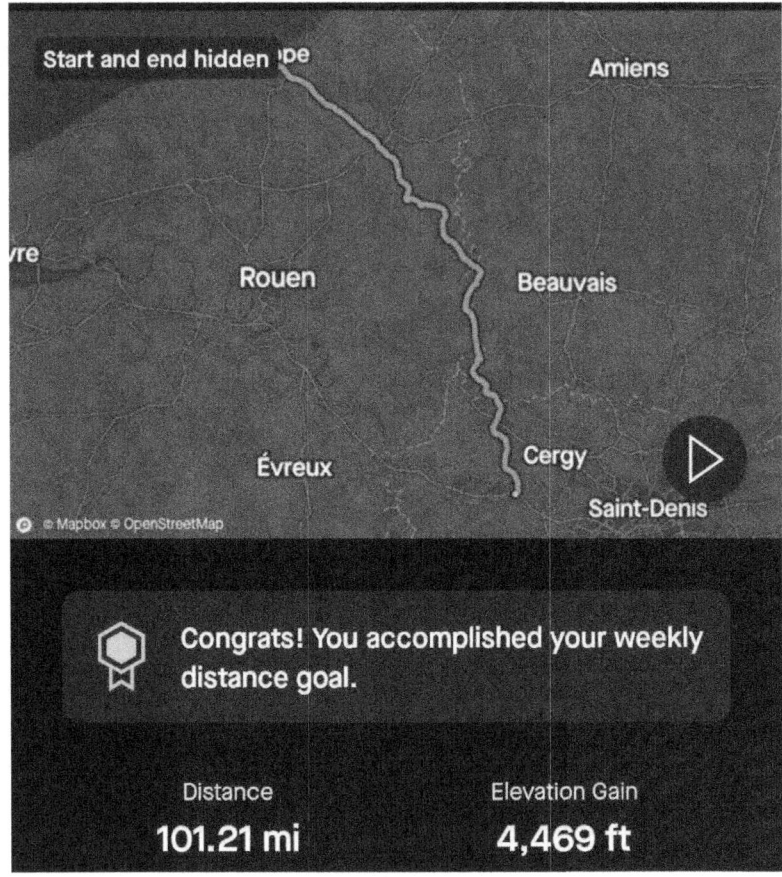

London 2 Paris Chapter 3: The Two (minus one) Towers

The accommodation gave seedy motel vibes.....probably because it was one. But the 8€ breakfast greatly exceeded our expectations. A Croissant, Pain-au-Chocolat and Bread. Yoghurt and Cereal. Good stuff. We'd got exceptionally lucky with the weather again. The whole trip not one drop of rain! If you'd added foul weather into the mix yesterday, I reckon that could have broken people. But the sun was on our side it seemed.

Today should have been a simple victory stroll into Paris. Snap a few pics in front of the tower full of eyes, then pop to Louis' (sort of our boss?) apartment for a free lunch. The way my Berlin trip "should" have ended. Still salty about that.

But I guess we spoke too soon. Spoke! SPoKE!!!!!... S P   O   K   E!!!! (haha. puns are funny. haha! :)) Wheeling Tim's bike into the car-park a rattling noise showed us he now had a broken spoke. I've literally never broken a road-bike spoke whilst riding, and it happens twice on this trip? Still clueless as to how it happened. Most likely someone attempting to move the bikes when a pedal was jammed in there. But could have been from hitting all the potholes. The 2mph tumble probably didn't help. Finding out why didn't help us anyway. We just had to deal with the "what now?". The "what now?" turned out to be boringly simple. Do absolutely nothing. Despite a missing spoke putting Martin's bike completely out of action...Tim's seemed pretty fine. The wheel was a bit wobbly, but was nowhere near the frame, and looked a lot worse than it rode.

So we followed the sage advice of "*If it's only slightly fucked. Don't try and fix it and risk increasing the fuckedness*". Cest la Vie and off we rolled.
There were lovely roads towards Paris. Cyclists outnumbering cars 20-to-1. This was THE place to be as a Parisian cyclist on a sunny, Sunday morning.

Some more beautiful routes through forests and we popped out in Versailles. Versailles has a palace, which is a bit of an understatement. It makes other palaces look like "quite nice houses. A good fixer-upper". It was ludicrously ostentatious and grand, it probably makes our queen incredibly jealous, which is probably why Louis went so hard on it.

We'd hoped to cycle through the massive grounds. But our way was blocked because the French still hadn't cleared up after the Olympics. Lazy!

A 30 minute detour around, but not in, the beautiful palace grounds and we got to the entrance.

I'm not going to describe Versailles too much. As really you should just go there and experience it yourself. It's surprisingly easy to reach from Paris. Super close and accessible. Just like Slough with London. Well worth the day trip. Versaille. Not Slough.

When we stopped for a coffee, I disappeared for a "worrying" amount of time. Perhaps in search of the famous "Treats of Versailles"? Every panicked phone call and message from Tim was ignored. Eventually I reappeared with 30 euros worth of brioche, biscuits, nuts and bottles of Crazy Tiger stuffed into every available crevice. Yes the biscuits were good, but nothing worth starting a world war over.

I'd gotten a bit carried away with how relaxing today was. We were now actually behind schedule, and going to be late for lunch. The horror.

So even the chilled day ended with a fairly full gas push to make up for lost time.

My eyes had been bigger than his pockets. Do you remember in the middle ages? When women wore those corsets and tops that made everyone look extremely busty? It was like that, just swapping cleavage for cakes. My special shorts were oozing cakes.

When hitting bumps, bottles and biscuits were being squeezed out of their hiding places. Zipping directly into the path of the gang, like mariokart, when you hold the back button before firing the green shells. Some deft swerving was required to avoid being catastrophically wiped out by a 2-litre water bottle. But thankfully Elena and Ollie were up to the task.

The gang reached Paris slightly late, but all in one piece. The route took a scenic path beside the Seine; a perfect view of the tower making a perfect ending. We had a brief rest and obligatory pics at the base of "Le Tower", in our now quite smelly Generic Finance Company tops. Then slaloming through the tourists to a fantastic and fitting feast at Louis' chic apartment. Louis had prepared a roast chicken. Elena was elated. There were many other courses as well. Obviously there was wine and cheese. Some berries and unnatural yoghurt to finish. Delicious. Many thanks to Louis and family for the food and a quality reward and send-off. Another feel-good factor: over the trip we had just edged over our goal of raising over £500 for Shave the

Children.

Certainly, here's a closing sentence that sums up the trip, "The cycling trip from London to Paris was a true test of endurance, filled with unexpected mishaps and challenges, but ultimately it was an unforgettable journey of resilience and determination and croissants."

Adventure complete, the gang, minus me, trundled off to train it & ferry home. I don't know what happened on the ferry back, other than it is a good bet that Elena ordered some more chicken (**editor note**: She later confirmed this to be the case). But apparently everyone got home safe. Shapo to everyone involved and those that supported and gave us virtual cheers and encouragement in Generic Finance Company Slack.

London 2 Paris 2 Calais

Chapter 4: The Sequel

Nobody Wanted, or Asked

For.

Like Frodo being asked to cast the ring into the fire[OBJ]. I wasn't done cycling. I'd been kind of jealous of the effort and challenge for the others, and wanted a piece of that feeling. This was another scenario where an idea had been planted in my head, and I just felt like seeing what happened. Daniel had been considering cycling back to Calais over two days, but noted that the French countryside between Paris and Calais was pretty mundane farmland.

So my logic went: "*if the views are shite...might as well ride at night!*" Genius. So at around 3pm I set off from Louis' apartment near the centre. I'd never done a proper overnight ride before. The closest I'd come was when I tried to get the ferry and cycle to Brielle (next to Rotterdam) in a single day. I'd got the 2am ferry from Dover to Dunkerque assuming I could grab enough sleep to make it bearable.

For whatever inexplicable reason, a Belgian school trip was also getting the 2am ferry back home...so I had two hours of coca-cola'd up children, running around screaming to contend with. Zero sleep, followed by a 130 mile cycle into a brutal Hook of Holland Headwind. After that incident I'd sworn off these silly sleep deprivation rides. A lot of audaxes (unofficial ultra distance bicycle road races) are multiday. And so to "win" you end up getting about 20mins sleep in a thin sleeping bag in a bush at the side of the road. No thanks. I love the long distance challenges, but learning about how important sleep is...I don't want to take multiple days of my precious lifespan...that is unless I can save £50 on accommodation by attempting to sleep on ferries.

Cycling through Paris is a nightmare. I've said that London is like Hanoi nowadays. Everyone out for themselves, pure chaos. Paris is maybe even slightly worse. Despite leaping between bike lane, bus lane, car lanes. Dodging clueless pedestrians and drivers alike, I somehow managed to get through Saint Denis, and the northern outskirts of Paris unscathed.

This was a fucked up ride. It really was pretty boring. It was about 200 miles from Paris to Calais, and although it'd been "steady" for me on the way to Paris...being on the bike nearly all-day, compared to sitting at a desk, still takes its toll. By the 50 mile mark I was a very tired boy. Also just jaded and not really into it. It really didn't help that I had my silly tailfin bag rather than panniers. It works a bit like the Bucking Bronco game. It works great, but then you load more and more stuff in it until you reach an invisible threshold. Then the weight will cause it to consistently deform itself, one section drooping down, flopping onto the rear wheel. This slows you down a bit, and both wears out the bag and the tyre. But the sound it makes is so aggravating, it is impossible to ignore. And no matter what you do with the straps, it'll keep doing this. So you have to choose between stopping every 40 minutes to deal with it...or redistributing contents to my backpack. Which I didn't want to do, as my shoulders ached and the straps were already digging in. Knowing the journey to Paris would be easy I'd avoided packing light, making it a bit more challenging. Plus I'd never explicitly committed to riding back. Even now, halfway there I still had the option of a train on the table. But knowing me, once I'd set off, I was going to see it through.

So I battled on. Starting a ride so late in the day is tough psychologically. Always recommend an early start. It was getting dark when I'd barely got out of Paris. Then Daniel was correct, I was just riding through vast fields. Way bigger than English ones, so you don't even get the pretty checkerboard patterns. Looking at the horizon up ahead, there were billows of smoke and countless flashing lights. What the flip is this? Turned out to be a multi-car pileup on a crossroads over a busy road. Hopefully people were ok. I don't know. I didn't want to rubberneck, just followed the police instructions, and went through the road closed sign and onwards into the night.

Around 10pm I was on the outskirts of Arrass, closing on 50% of the distance down...but most of the elevation was still ahead. As I smelt the alluring scent of dirty late night fast-food joints, Mr Lizard took the reins. One of my out-of-body "I don't remember planning to get off the bike here" experiences. Despite being a so-called vegetarian, I found myself stopping at the first kebab shop on Arrass outskirts. Ordering a chicken burger and greasy fries flooded with mayo. Wolfing it down like a starving...wolf. Get it in my mouth quick. Get it in my stomach quick. (**editor note**: You've probably noticed what a ridiculous amount of meat I eat for a vegetarian. I'm doing a lot better at that nowadays. I was a bit too hyperfocussed on "got to get my recommended protein intake", scared that my legs would wither away if I went a single day without sufficient grams. It certainly takes a lot more preparation and forethought vegging it through many places…should be lucky that it's even possible around Western Europe.)

I hadn't ruled out the possibility that I would randomly stop and get a last minute hotel. However deep down I'd only be proud of myself if I "one-rided it"…also I'd only taken a half day off work on the Monday. My manager had booked me in for a 2pm meeting the following day, so that kind of forced my hand.

I kept cycling post-burger. Once it hit midnight, it felt like the ride was do-able, and at this point, getting a hotel would just be silly. I bonked around 30 minutes later.

1:30AM, just outside Bernaville, I spy some lights off the side of the road. Intrigued. It was an abandoned/closed petrol station, but there was a weird small lighted building just off to the side of it. Maybe a vending machine? I didn't have enough food to get me to Calais and my body was yearning for calories, so I pulled in to check it out. It was a flipping pizza vending machine….at 1:30am in the middle of nowhere. The pizza on the sign looked delicious. What came out was an abomination. Yet somehow a tasty abomination. The black olives looked like they'd been forged in the fires of mount doom. The cheese anaemic and not thoroughly melted. Cheap ham. Dodgy mushrooms….yet it tasted amazing. Would highly recommend if you're in the area. The area of Bernaville where there's nothing to do. You've got to savour the little victories when you're low, and this significantly lifted my spirits.

Good job too, as around 2am, when it really was too silly to hotel it...the rain came. Slow pitter-patter at first, but crescendoing throughout the night. It ebbed away and back on at points, but by the time I was getting off my bike it was a full-on downpour. Never put my raincoat on. Pushing too hard, would have just cooked.

3am the tiredness started getting scary. Like: *"I'll just have some microsleeps where I close my eyes for 2 seconds. I'm sure nothing bad will happen."* No cars or people around. Nothing to see at the roadside. My brain was numb. At least I'd finally given up on the tailfin bag, moved some of the heavy stuff to my rucksack. No more aggravating fiddling with straps. I had my powerbank stowed in the frame-bag, and attached a cable snaking to the light on the handlebars, keeping it just about powered throughout the night.

I was so tired I couldn't safely eat whilst riding. I had to stop, or I'd just wobble off the road. At one point, around 4:30am, when I stopped to eat an oat-bar. I decided to have a mini-lay down under a relatively dry oak tree. There were strange scuttling sounds and the breaking of branches nearby in the woods. A big animal. But that didn't stop me from closing my eyes for 5-10 minutes. It really was nothing, pretty sure I didn't sleep, but even just that closing of eyes did wonders. Gave me a small mental boost and recovery. I started having a bit more fun. Or I'd just completely lost it. Yelled "Bonjourno" to some people awake for whatever reason by the side of the road with a car.

Heard them yelling loudly in French back. No idea what. Got spooked imagining them hopping in the car, track me down, bury me in the woods. I cycled slightly faster.

Nobody murdered me and I finally reached the national-park area South of Calais, indicating that I'm nearly there...well at least 30 or 40 miles out. And areas of beauty == areas of hilly. But that feels do-able. I really, really, really, really wanted to be home. As soon as possible. I calculated if I smashed it at superhuman speed I could make the 7:30am ferry. If I missed it, the next one was after 9am. So like with nearly every trip approaching a ferry, smashing time commenced. I went into my super-saiyan stomping on the pedals mode I'd mastered over the year.

What I mean about mastering the stompy style? The common advice for ultra-distance cycling is to take it as easy as possible, stay seated, tap the pedals, avoid big power. But I'd had to forgo this advice on the Berlin ride. The obnoxiously heavy bike seemed to be more efficient if you tried to use its weight against itself. If I whipped the bike around and jumped on the pedals, it felt like I was using my legs less, and gravity more. You could dance your way up hills far faster than the bike had any right to.

...well it turned out this style still applies to conventional road bikes for me. I may be an outlier, got a very un-cyclist like upper body. Used to do gym stuff before cycling, and never really lost the muscle. Not body-buildery, but definitely not cyclist bird-chested. If I stand up and blast it up hills (maybe not into zone 6, but at least zone5), then it feels like I'm climbing with my glutes, calves and upper body. Not using my quads. And riding the flats for hundreds of miles annihilates my quads first...so using this aggressive, silly hill climbing style…manages to distribute the load of the 200 mile ride more evenly over my whole body's muscles.

I was literally blazing up these hills staying above 15mph, going into the red, despite no sleep, and so many miles in my legs. "*Holy shit! The human body is pretty incredible when it wants to be in a warm comfy bed.*". The rain played its part. Mr Motivator. Feels more epic to be absolutely pounding it in the rain. And I guess the faster you go, the faster it's over xD
It looked like I was gonna make the 7:30 ferry, but it fell apart within 15 miles of the end. There were two reaaallly long hills right before the end, which finished me off physically. I gave up and took a few minutes break at the top. I wish I'd realised there was a humongous stretch of

downhill coming, which I blasted at 30mph average for a couple of miles. This renewed my hope, only to have it dashed again. I'd tried to replot a more direct route. This more direct route had a "short" "cut". It started off as a gravelly bike-path. That's rideable. I'm sure it won't be too long. The path turned slightly rougher. Still rideable. The path turned into a dirt path…errr, just about rideable. Eventually the path became a literally grassy field. Just a line of mud, one bike-tyre wide. On road tyres I was sliding all over the place at 5mph. Fuck this. It didn't even seem to be leading anywhere sensible. Just more off-road. So I double back, and with the time I'd lost, the dream was almost definitely dead.

There's still a window between checkin closing and ferry leaving where they can often be lenient with cyclists. I'd been at a heartrate of 150 for most of the ferry-chase. So I was curious as to whether I could keep it so high, so late into the ride. It was fun to keep going fast. So I kept going fast. You never know. Maybe I'm lucky. But another wrong turn in Calais meant I arrived at the ticket gate at 7:34, 4 minutes after the ferry had definitely left. Cest la vie. Look on the bright side. No stress dashing through the port. A relaxing coffee in the Calais lounge. Time to savour the accomplishment. At 200 miles, my first, and almost certainly last, overnight megaride.

Feck riding home from Dover. Got the train. Had a shower. To make it less likely I'd fall asleep, I took my laptop into a cafe. Fell asleep 10 times into the team meeting. Once you've fallen asleep once on webcam, you don't want to turn the cam off, as then it seems like you're probably asleep the whole time. Also the cafe is a cinema. Maybe your local cinema's are shite. But Canterbury has a nice quiet one, with lovely comfy chairs, lots of plug sockets, 10% discount on coffees if you are a member. It's also late into the evenings. I'm telling you, cinemas are better cafes than cafes.

(**note to editor**: Think of an entertaining way to sum up this chapter, rather than rambling about fucking cinemas as cafes. Wtf dude. Clearly getting lazy towards the end. [**editor note**: I can't be bothered either!])

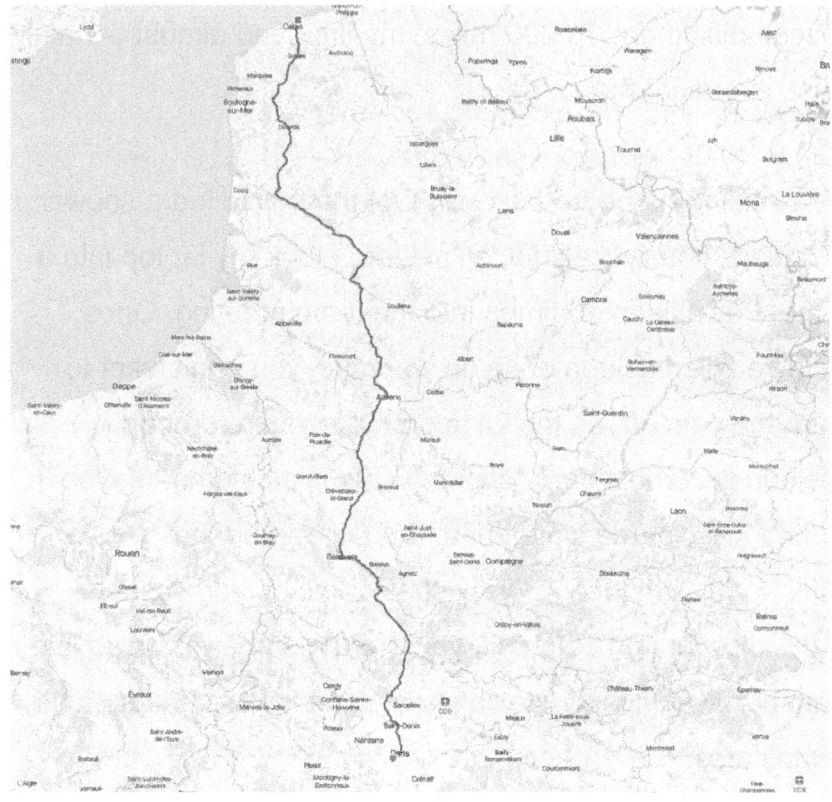

Interlude 3 or 4. I've lost count. Just fucking read it.

Receiving a phone call just after lunch in the bustling London office:

- Ello, Johnny
- ....
- Yeah
- ....
- Oh
- ....
- This Friday?
- ....
- Arrrrr...I can't, I'm err....in Japan right now :|
- ....
- mmmm
- ....
- Nah, Osaka
- ....
- Smaller than Tokyo yeah
- ....
- Dunno, Different
- ....

- Nah I wont be back in time

- ….

- mmmm

- ….

- yeah

- ….

- I know, I know. But I'm sure there'll be more funerals.

- ….

- No you're right. Not for him.

- ….

- I dunno, I'll do a toast to him in the bar tonight.

- ….

- errr, to the other people in the bar I guess.

- ….

- No I don't speak Japanese.

- ….

- Yes I know it was a dumb idea. I was just trying to soften how bad it is that I'm gonna miss it. But I'm not forking out over a grand on a last minute flight. Capiche?

- ….

- ….

- <sigh> Well can't you just put him in the freezer until I'm back?

- ….

- Why not?

- ….

- Alright, well anyway, I've gotta go. I hope it's a good sendoff.

- He was some turtle.

- ….

- I love you too. Bye :)

Ireland: The Final Adventure

Spoiler alert: Final as in "final of the year". Not my life. I
didn't die, as far as I'm aware. But boy (hehe butt-boy) was
it a fitting finale.

I love stoning multiple birds. And this year it felt like the
universe was pointing me towards The Emerald Isle:
- All my favourite Irish music artists were releasing stuff this
year (Fontaines DC, Kneecap, Sprints, And so I watch you
from afar, Not fight like apes...but I'd rediscovered how
much I loved them!)
- My Granny plays the penny whistle in Irish music sessions
and is a big fan of the place. I'd been trying to visit her a bit
more often this year. But we'd run out of things to talk
about....tangent: this is a good reason to write stuff down.
Now that I'm thinking about it, it seems obvious to bring
round a game of scrabble (or something slightly less boring
than scrabble).
- I was pretty proud of my no-air-travel streak. Ireland was
somewhere do-able with train & ferry. Keep the streak
going. But still felt exotic.
   - I know I can't keep it up indefinitely. I'm craving some
sunny cycling action next winter.

- I'd been wanting to climb Snowdon. It's a long way from Kent to Snowdon just to walk up and down a big hill…but it is right next to the ferry to Ireland!

- If you remember Gary who I wouldn't shut up about earlier in the book…"*Stop being a whiny emo and get to the cycling!*"…oh you do? Well I hadn't really gotten over her. I ended up comparing every other potential breeding-buddy to her, and none came out too favourably. I'm around that age where 70% of women are searching for suppliers of sperm to construct new humans. I don't like to time-waste. So that's a big chunk of the pussy-pool* gone. So the final number of fish in the sea, or at least fish I actually want to fuck, is depressingly small…which due to obscene overpopulation and unsustainable fishing practices is actually pretty accurate. I wasn't yet panicking, but I was certainly worrying. Was this going to be a long-term problem? So my creative solution was, if Gary is Irish….maybe Ireland is just full of beautiful and funny women?

Spoiler: It's not. Dogs the lot of them… (joke!). But maybe the Ireland trip would restore my faith in romance. Spoiler: It kind of did.

(**editor note**: "breeding-buddy". "pussy-pool". "fuckable fish". Dude you can't leave this shit in here surely? Just because someone has never used a phrase before, doesn't make it worth using. I know it's got alliteration, but it doesn't make you look clever. It just makes you look like a horny, edgy 14 year old)

One of those many reasons may have been stronger than others...but either way, it felt like the Universe was pushing me towards Ireland and it feels comfortable to let yourself get swept along by the flow of the Universe. So off we go!

The Plan:
- Train up to Bangor on Thursday evening after work
- Up Snowdon early on Friday.
- Ferry to Dublin on Saturday.
- Big night out in Dublin, then a mega-cycle from Dublin, all the way to Galway on the West coast.
- 4 (or 5?) nights in Galway. It's a great central point for doing day trips from. One day ride up the coast north. Another day to the lakes. Inish Mor on another day. (Originally it was going to be a longer epic trip, each night in a separate place...but it's more relaxing to get settled in one place. And branch out on day trips.)
- Galway to Limerick via the Burren and Cliffs of Moher.

- Small ride out from Limerick, train from Limerick Junction to Kildare. Back to Dublin through the Wicklow mountains in time for the 2am ferry
- Ferry back to Holyhead on Anglesey. Looong train all the way home.

First, let's get this final adventure off to a banger with some boringly sensible and useful travel information. Woooh! I wasn't aware of this for my trip, but if you search for "sailrail ireland", turns out there's combined ferry+train tickets to get between Dublin and most UK citiies, which are only about £60 each way. It's so suspiciously cheap I was sure it was a scam at first. It doesn't give you a bike reservation on the Avanti trains, but I feel like you can just phone them up and get one. If you're looking to do Ireland on a budget and hate flying with bikes, or just hate flying in general…"sailrail" is well worth investigating.

Whilst we're being boring, it's tough to get cold, hard data on ferry emissions. It has to account for all the transport lorries, and then there's peak season vs off-season. Travelling in the less busy off-season is technically "higher emissions per person"….but the ferry is going with or without you, so… ‾_(ツ)_/‾. Depending on mysterious and complex "factors", going alone in your car really doesn't seem much better than flying. But I'm 99% sure foot and bike passengers…unless you weigh as much as a small car…definitely have a considerably lower footprint than air travel.

I could have taken the fancy road bike. I wanted to rack up big miles to see as many sights as possible. But I was a bit burnt from the London handlebar snafu. Knowing I was staying overnight in Dublin, I googled: "*Where's the safest place to leave a nice bike in Dublin*". Top answer: "*Nowhere*"….brilliant. Guess I'm not taking the Ribble.

Plus, hotels in Ireland are pretty pricey. The only reasonably priced accommodation left in Galway, airbnb style house, didn't seem like a "bike inside" kind of place. I'd started the year with a crazy cycle on San: The sluggish Schwinn granny-bike. So it felt fitting, kind of symmetrical, to end the year on it as well.

Earlier I'd called it Lucy, because you know, Loosey...due to all the loose bolts. But it really is such a dull name. No offence to people called Lucy. If anything it makes me more impressed by your accomplishments. But I've never heard of a revolutionary called Lucy, or a titan of industry. It's just not the kind of name to associate with an epic steed, being ridden on grand adventures. So nowadays I call it San. For reasons that will become clearer later.

San had not been serviced since Berlin. I'd fiddled about with the brakes a bit to try and get them to work stronger. The kickstand was still duck-taped to the frame to stop it wobbling about. Pedalling caused the bottom-bracket to make a faint grindy sound. Didn't sound healthy, but had it always sounded like that? It was built from cheap-as-chips components.

For this trip I'd been sensible and said "fuck the tent". My sleep had been so poor in tents on the Berlin trip, that I didn't want to ruin my last big trip of the year. It was hotels all the way! Well hotels or houses...or hostels...or ferries...but no fecking tents!

Despite no tent or sleeping gear, the bike was somehow nearly as heavy as Berlin. With the idea that I might try and talk to women at some point, only having sweaty cycling gear didn't sound ideal.

Chaos before the trip even commenced. I arrived at Euston amid carnage. The gates were shut, not letting anybody in. Meaning there were hordes of people jammed up outside.

I'd walked my bike halfway into the mob…and now there was no space to retreat out, against the flow of people. I managed to clamber up some steps and get the bike out of the way. Stood it up against a costa coffee wall, also giving a good vantage point to survey the scene.

Nobody seemed to have much idea of what was going on. Somebody said cyberattack. Somebody said people on lines. Somebody said leaves on lines. Whatever cause, it seemed literally every train was fubar. Nothing in or out. I was supposed to be on the 7pm train, arriving in Bangor about 10:20pm. I'd arrived an hour early to avoid stress, so there was still ample time, but it was concerning: what would happen if no more trains went to Bangor tonight? My schedule was pretty tight. I'd already booked the Dublin ferry on Saturday. So if I didn't get to Wales tonight, Snowdon would have to be a No-don…

Half an hour later the gates were finally opened and people streamed into the station. The trains were all still just getting delayed or cancelled. It's a pain being in these kind of situations with fully-loaded bikepacking setups. If you pop to get food, or to the toilet…you come back to staff or police swarming over your bike. Treating you like an imbecile for daring to leave it unoccupied for 2 minutes. I'm sorry, I guess I forgot to just turn my bladder off? Or do you want me to go in a bottle?

Around 7 some other trains started running. Not mine. But at least something was happening. It felt like a gameshow, or watching the lottery draw: "*Arriving at Platform 7 is the……*". C'mon!!!! Alas the winning trains were always someone else's. Never Bangor. By 8:30pm I'd stress-eaten 3 luxury toasts. It feels a bit cheeky for Starbucks to describe them as luxury, but there genuinely does feel something luxury about tucking into a nice piece of hot buttered toast on a train home.

Finally, finally, on the 15th? announcement, it was Bangor time. There was panic in the air, the clusterfuck had meant that seat reservations were probably all over the place. People wanted to be first on to get seats, as well as ensuring they got on what could be the final train home by this time. I got caught up in their panic. It was not helped by the train car letters seeming to have no relation to where in the train they were. So I was dashing to and fro up the platform like a trapped mouse, desperately trying to find the cycle-carriage car for my bike.

I found the cycle car and boarded. We pulled away around 9:40pm. Phew. I chilled out in the area by the doors for a while to de-stress. Then went searching for my seat. The journey was unremarkable once going...until about the halfway mark. An attendant coming through the train informed everyone that because we were so late, they would have already started engineering work on the line north of Crewe...errr which means what?

It meant rail replacement buses from Crewe to all the potential finishing points. I had very little faith in the train company pulling off a last minute rail replacement bus system effectively. So I searched out some crew and asked how it was going to work. Had they done the numbers on the number of passengers, and would people have to wait for Buses to do round trips? Would it take all night? It was 98 miles from Crewe to Bangor. A pretty insane cycle starting at 11pm in the piddling rain. But fresh off the Calais madness, it didn't seem that crazy...and it would be less frustrating having something to do, rather than sitting waiting in Crewe until 5am.

But the staff assured me: "*Don't worry. We've done the numbers. There'll be enough buses for everyone.*". Oh good.

As approximately 400 people filed out of Crewe station into the car park....there was 1 bus. 1 bus. For 400 people. Great.

The initial bus was actually a proper coach, with a big luggage undercarriage. So it could have taken my bike. But I was in no rush and didn't need to be one of the lucky few who got on the first bus.

Turns out I was in the minority. Everyone else pushed and barged their way on. Once the bus was completely full, it was noticed that none of the people with small kids had made it.

Parents having to fiddle with pushchairs. Or the children slowing them down with their short, slow legs. Some of the parents were noticeably not amused. Apparently they hadn't brought any baby food with them. I felt this demonstrated a far greater level of trust in the British railway system than was sensible. The "head train guy" went onboard the bus and asked if anybody would be willing to give up their seat for the families with small children. And maybe it was the "train guy's" young face and nervous demeanour…but hats off to the passengers. The whole bus reverse Spartacus'd it. Nobody stood up. Nobody offered. They all sat their ground. Pretended not to hear. Brave warriors.

So eventually bus #1 left. Leaving most people waiting. The train guy balancing frantically calling anyone who owned a bus, whilst fending off a barrage of questions and abuse from the angry remainders.

The train guy's phone calls end up delivering us a hodgepodge of vehicles. Each one resembling less and less of a bus. Down to minibuses and large vans. It's the Dunkirk of our generation. These tired, grumpy drivers saving us from the horrors of a night in Crewe.

The chaos of the train system breakdown seems like it could be a short, 7/10-on-imdb, low-budget independent film. It would be described as "Quintessentially British". I'm not usually into people-watching as much as others enjoy it. Also last time the police confiscated my binoculars. But it's so dramatic. There's people with dogs. Lads being sick. People battling with leads to stop said dog eating said sick. People striking up temporary friendships and chats with nothing else to do, brought together by the failings of our transport system. Like virtual particles and antiparticles flashing into existence in the vacuum, getting to know each other, then parting forever. Well the particle-pair annihilates themselves which doesn't really apply here. This metaphor is going off the rails. Haha.

As the buses were getting less and less bussy, there was nothing suitable to carry my bike in. So it was just me and a couple of others left. Another passenger had bought his girlfriend in Bangor a new bike as a present (which looked suspiciously like mine, just with a front basket). It was me and him, plus a third who lived by one of those middle-of-nowhere stations, where no driver could be bothered diverting to. I probably should have just cycled it, but the scenario had been so entertaining, that it was worth hanging around and seeing how it resolved.

How was it resolved? I ended up in a 98 mile taxi journey from Crewe to Bangor at 2am. Hats off to Avanti for ensuring everyone got to their destination. They even paid for the taxi upfront so there was no need for us to reimburse.

Tried to kip on the drive. Maybe managed a brief nap, some slight shut-eye at best. Pretty sure the driver was falling asleep too. He kept weirdly leaning forwards really far, like he was trying to shake himself awake.

When I engaged him in conversation to try and keep him awake, he immediately drifted right onto the hard shoulder. We were fractions of a second from being in the grass when he noticed. And he noticed with a jolt. He panicked, panicked hard! He swerves, skidding all the way to the other side of the motorway. "*Sorry about that*".
"*Errr...yeah.*" I didn't speak for the rest of the trip, except for the one time he tried to turn the wrong way into a one way street.

The hotel just outside Bangor, The Slate, had been very helpful and provided clear instructions for getting in via a lockbox, sticking the bike in the breakfast area, and then getting to my room. Nice hotel and got a decent amount of sleep. Quality breakfast as well.

Ireland Day 2: Erm…actually…this is Wales not Ireland? Snowdon…more like Snowup :|

Headed out at 9 in the morning. I had been apprehensive about taxi'ing my bike. To fit it in the boot, I'd disconnected the front brakes so the wheel could be taken off. There was always the risk that I wouldn't be able to connect it back correctly. This is a really simple job. But I'm a really simple person. At the time I didn't really have an alternative option, it seemed alright as I rolled off down the road.

We rode through Snowdonia to the base of the Llanberris ascent path. The ride was enjoyable with the anticipation and excitement of the day ahead. Snowdonia is a bit hilly, ya don't say? But the roads were fairly quiet on a Friday morning.

There's multiple routes up Snowdon. Llanberris is the "simplest". I'd considered trying other routes, however the forecast was a tad windy, with showers to make things slippy. My trainers are held together with duct-tape. The soles already worn and smoothed. Too sketchy to attempt one of the tougher ascents. Especially on my own, no help if something went wrong.

So I kept it simple with Llanberris. I was worried that it was going to be too easy. That it would just be a glorified big hill. They say nearly anyone can climb Snowdon, and hearing that it can be done in a few hours…sounds really easy. But all that walking is uphill. Very little downhill on the ascent to the mountain summit. Quel surpris. Starts off steep to drain your legs. Levels out a bit; here you can see the top, the surroundings become very open and exposed. The wind starts to bite. Layers are added. Higher up, the trail turns into big stones. You hop over, or up, it gets steep again at some point. More stone. I was worried the showers meant I'd get up there and the visibility would be dire. Fortunately the clouds were hovering around the summit but not lower. You could see all the way back down into the valleys below. Lovely. The showers made momentary, but still exquisite rainbows.

What a great walk. Approaching the top my fear of heights was kicking in. The path got a bit narrower, when you try it you'll probably think "*how is this scary?*"…but if you don't like heights, and have an overactive imagination...you can picture a massive gust of wind, blowing you 6 feet sideways, tumbling far, far down. No more pics nearer the top, scared the wind would catch my phone and send it into the void. Also, fuck taking my gloves off in that cold.

I was overtaking people and dashing the last small section to the top. Combination of excitement and the height thing. At the top there is a tiny stone "monument" looking thing, the official summit. Most people were going up to touch it, taking a selfie or two. It felt like I had to touch the tip as well. Come all this way. So I trudged up the final steps. But as I did, it felt like the wind kicked into overdrive. I've never been blown so hard. I felt like I couldn't even stand up. Crouching down I pathetically reached out my fingertip like E.T., and just poked the tip. Then slunk down the steps on my hands and feet like some diabolical creature. Feet first, belly up. Hands on the ground behind me. Must have looked ridiculous. Especially because no-one else was doing this, they were just walking like normal humans. I don't understand, maybe I just greatly overestimate the effect of wind. Maybe it comes from cycling, where gusts of wind can send your bike many feet from where you want it to be. I reckon that statistically, the closest I've been to death was cycling down windy mountains in Gran Canaria.

Being an island, with zero trees, the wind is substantial. On a lightweight carbon bike, with ridiculous deep, aero rims...the gusty winds would literally move you ¾ of the way across the road. And it seemed like the harder you tried to turn back to your side of the road...the stronger the wind got. Despite turning with all your might, your bike would just remain right in the middle of the road. Staring into the headlights of an oncoming car, feeling like you can't get back to your side of the road is...slightly frightening, and has probably led to a life-long fear of wind.

The cafe at the top was reasonably priced. It's literally at the top of a mountain. Where else are you gonna go? It's nice that they don't take the piss. Always kind of sours an experience when your mood is jolly, and you think "*This is really nice. Why go home yet. Let's stay and have a coffee!*"....and then it's fecking £5 for a piddly little cup. Feels like you're being mugged, and your perfect day is ruined. So yeah, it was lovely to get a hot chocolate for about £3, which I could dip my "reduced as going out-of-date" tea-cakes into.

Worth walking down as well. When you're walking up, you're primarily looking up at Snowdon, and have to keep doing 360 spins to catching the awesome views of the valleys. Going down gives you more time to look down. It's also interesting comparing the people you meet going up in the late morning. With the people you meet ascending in the later afternoon. Erm...yeah, good luck to you, you poorly prepared afternoon adventurers!

Nearer the base, it started proper pelting it. So I popped into the pub a short way up the route. Very odd place. Nice, I think. The owner just had a quirky sense of humour I think. Oldy-woldy, with a proper fireplace, which I ended up sat on a sofa in front of. Quiet, no music, just hushed talking, shifting of coats and crackling of fire. There was a massive body-buildery type guy there who'd buggered his knee near the start, patiently waiting for friends to come back down. But apart from that everyone else seemed local. Either just local, local, or Snowdon "volunteers". Not proper mountain rescue, but I guess they do litter-picking, path maintenance, that kind of invisible work that you never think about, but would greatly appreciate if the people doing it suddenly didn't. Everyone was speaking in Welsh, which obviously is fine, it's Wales. But it does seem like one of the most demonic sounding languages to me. Like if you told me that the Devil was real, and that he lived in Rhyl...I would not be in the least bit surprised. I smashed my latte pretty quick, paid and went on. After I explained I was travelling by bicycle and didn't have a car, the owner bid me farewell with "enjoy your drive". Odd sense of humour. Back on the bike and started cycling back the way I came, north, through Bangor, and most of the way across Anglesey. Tonight I was staying in a village called Valley, close enough that you could wake up at a reasonable time, and still cycle for the 10am ferry from Holyhead → Dublin.

Great cycling from Snowdon back to Bangor. Grey skies but still soaking in the warm feeling from the adventure. To get across the water from Bangor into Anglesey, the route attempted to take me on a dual-carriageway. I wasn't having that, so hopped off and had to walk half a kilometre back to the roundabout exit. Rode to the other side of Bangor and headed across the more sensible and prettier small bridge. As you look to your left on this bridge, you can see some guy, or girl, but most probably an unhinged guy...sorry if that's sexist...anyway whatever gender...they have built their house slap bang in the middle of the massive river, the one separating Anglesey from the rest of Wales. Looks totally badass. Also totally impractical. You'd need a boat to go literally anywhere, even to just pop to shops for a pint of milk. How do you get your post? So many questions.

As I was literally riding through Anglesey I stopped and took a pic of the Llanfairpwllgwyngyllgogerychwyrndrobwllllantysiliogogogoch railway station sign. Llanfairpwllgwyngyllgogerychwyrndrobwllllantysiliogogogoch kind of annoys me really. Yeah it's funny when Welsh places have long, unpronounceable names...but I dunno, this one just feels somehow too long to be funny. Llanfairpwllgwyngyllgogerychwyrndrobwllllantysiliogogogoch, it's just taking the joke too far. Trying way too hard. Grow up.

The rest of the route across Anglesey to Valley was shite. We were following one of the main, straight roads to make it quick. Which was silly because there was tonnes of time to spare. It was a menacing headwind and lumpy-bumpy as fuck. Which always feels worse on a busy, boring road. Tired legs, struggling, slow pace. Made me a bit scared about the days ahead. Dublin to Galway was going to be rough if I got a headwind like this. (**editor note**: Did I just forget that I'd climbed all the way up Snowdon, and that might have used up quite a bit of energy?)

If you cycle through Anglesey, I recommend avoiding these main central roads. Take the prettier, smaller coast roads and just give yourself a bit more time.

But we got there eventually. A rudimentary but passable hotel above a pub. Grabbed fish and chips, some heavily reduced cheese & onion rolls and made sure I got an early night after last night's 2am taxi trip.

Ireland Day 1: Dublin Debacle

Up the next morning, I'd learnt my lesson. Took the beautiful coastal roads up to Holyhead. There's a lovely bridge just outside Valley, where you get an incredibly picturesque view of Snowdonia in the distance. The early morning sun shining rays down on it through gaps in the clouds. A little boat out on the river in the foreground. Top notch food for the eyes.

Taking the scenic route, I hadn't left much leeway for checkin time. Minor panic. I'd managed to drop my "final destination" route pin, 1 metre the wrong side of a massive fence enclosing the port. So by the time I realised I was on the wrong side, and there was no-way through the thin chain fence. I had to time-trial it back Remco style, doing about 18mph average on San, all the way back into Holyhead, following the road signs for car ferry to the other side of the fence.

The ferry security going to Ireland seems tighter than France. There was an x-ray scanner machine for foot passengers luggage. Oh shit. What about the explosive can of GT-85 in my bag? Welp, shouldn't have feared at all. I'm a cyclist after all. I am above the law. They waved me, my bike, and my bag with the explosive material straight on through.

Ferry was uneventful. People have told me horror stories of the Irish Sea, maybe I just got lucky. Wicklow mountains on the approach to Dublin loomed aggressively. Looked taller than I'd imagined. Tall for me and San anyway. Upon debarking, one of the crew was hoovering the floor and had the hoover strapped to his chest and back. Looked like a ghostbuster. Maybe this was just a part-time gig. Maybe there weren't enough ghosts to earn a full time living from busting? Once you've sucked all the ghosts, you've got to wait for more deaths with unfulfilled souls, so until then I guess you go bust some dust to pay the mortgage.

Dublin port is fecking massive. Takes about 15 minutes to cycle out of it. Not a brilliant first impression to be honest. However at the very first pedestrian crossing outside the port, I got talking to a couple of lads. One was keen on cycling, both very friendly. I'd only been in Ireland 15 minutes and already someone had asked: "*D'ya wan' ta come ta moi place for a cuppa tae?*"

I really wish I'd said yes. Usually I'll say yes to anything spontaneous, I'm an insurance salesman's wet dream. Yet I'm simultaneously loath to suddenly deviate from formulated plans. With Gary bombarding me with Dublin tips, I kind of had the whole day aggressively planned out. No space left in the schedule to account for the friendliness of Irish people and chance cups of tea. In hindsight a mistake, but we all have to live with our mistakes and move on. Just learn and choose the correct call next time.

I'd signed up for a candle painting class at 2:30pm. Yes a candle painting class; and I didn't want to turn up late. I could tell the guy was a bit disappointed and hurt by my tea refusal. About 50 metres down the road, I had a really strong urge to 180, ask if the tea offer was still on the table. Alas, I kept cycling onwards, the fun adventure missed.

Why was I at a candle painting class? Especially one so vitally important to trigger punctuality anxiety? Well, it was because the Tote-bag painting class was sold out...are you happy with that explanation? No? Ok then. So when Gary looked up events happening in Dublin that weekend, up popped tote-bag painting. I've done zilch painting in about 20 years, anything artistic really. I was curious as to how it would go. Would I still have the skills of a five-year-old? Would my creativity shine through despite this? The venue's top picture on google maps hooked me even harder. No joke, it's a sculpture of a gigantic brown dog turd. Not even an artistic or impressively detailed turd either. Just an amateur turd. Such a strange and bad thing to have as the top picture, now I had to go! Surely this would be a bit more fun than the usual tourist museum malarkey.

The place was on the edge of Temple Bar, where all the stumbling stags and hens roam after dark, emptying their innards into the local sewers. I swung by the nearby famous Trinity college grounds first. As I was locking my bike up, once again I was subjected to a friendly conversation. Against my will; with an older, fast-talking woman, who was locking her bike up next to mine. Commiserating about the state of bicycle thefts in Dublin. Next to us was a folding bike...or what used to be a folding bike. It looked like someone had sawn it in half to bypass the lock...but then realised that a sawn-in half bike is not very useful...so just left it. So after having my ear talked off (in a good way), I eventually decided against locking my bike up there, heeded her advice, and locked it up inside the Trinity grounds. Trinity college is nice old buildings, nice bits of green grass. Reminds me of the architecture from the classic videogame Gears of War, where you lay as a bulky man who has a chainsaw strapped to his machine gun, which you use to tear aliens in half from the groin upwards. Beautiful stuff. No pics but it's probably on google street view. Still an active university, so it must be a tad odd being a student there...all these tourists waddling round gawping and snapping. As someone perpetually late to lectures, it would have driven me mad trying to slalom through the slow crowds. Guess you get used to it.

Post Trinity stroll I was en-route to the painting. Inevitably early, so I paused to listen to a minor, impromptu United Against Racism rally. Don't know why, just seemed interesting. It's nice to know that other countries have racism too, not just us. The protest was about the police behaviour at a yearly culture night bloc party in temple bar. It had always been fine in previous years. But this year the Garda had cracked down on it with a heavy hand. Hate-crimes against immigrants have been rising in Dublin, leaving people peeved with the Garda for their impotence on that matter, yet somehow tremendously effective at pulverising a peaceful celebration. When I'd learned enough and was about to head off, chanting started. Felt a tad weird leaving at that exact moment. Also felt weird for a distinctly English sounding bloke joining in. So I lip-synced for a bit, then wandered off to the candle-painting building. Turned out it shared the building with an escape room. I had accidentally joined an escape room group. Once I realised this, I quickly snuck out the door; maybe that makes me the winner? Finally found the correct room.

The candle painting was…interesting.

The teacher showed us a couple of examples of large, fat candles with big diameters, fairly easy to paint on. Wow, look how professional they can look!

We were then given long, thin, spindly candles, way more difficult.
Teacher is the wrong word. She was a small, bubbly, elderlyish Italian woman. The "teaching" amounted to: "*This is paint. These are brushes. Paint goes on the candle. Good luck*".

We set to work. If you weren't careful, you'd rub and smudge your designs before they'd had time to dry. So I enquired: "How long does the paint take to dry?". "*A long time. Hours*"

"That's very inconvenient"

"*Yes it is. Good luck*".

I was sat with a pair of young ladies, plus another couple. The boyfriend had very clearly been dragged there by his girlfriend. He seemed ecstatic that someone had showed up with whom he could talk football with. He genuinely spent about 10 minutes of the 2 hours painting. He confessed to me he was a Manchester City supporter. I could have told you that from his finished candles. Uninspired and soulless.

"Are you just bitter because he spent 10 minutes and his candles still looked more professional than yours? And you could probably put his in a candle-selling shop and people wouldn't notice...but if we put your candle in a shop people would go 'wtf is this. Why has someone brought their own shit candle and put it in this shop of proper candles?" ......

Maybe I am just bitter...but candle-painting shouldn't be about professionalism. It shouldn't be about straight lines and unsmudged colours. It should be transferring your emotions and feelings to the candle. Before you proceed to burn them away. Although I highly recommend not burning these candles. I would not be the least surprised if these paints gave off fumes toxic to humans. I could still probably give one of my Granny anyway. Her method of "recycling plastic" is to throw it on the fire. I was incredulous when this happened and was treated as "normal". So compared to that, a little bit of acrid oil-paint fumes is no bother.

Where did my inspiration come from? Mice and bicycles both mean a lot to me. The mice that live in my shed, the closest creatures to pets that I have. Then San, who has fared me well throughout these grand adventures. Combined that with some Irish green grass. Some random squiggles for additional flair. And walla! Cest Magnifique! Having expended my creativity budget, on the second candle I did a slapdash Tesco logo and wrote "**Help. I have no idea what I'm doing!**".

My paper doodles had been worryingly distant from their intended shapes, yet the mouse and bike actually came out surprisingly decent. Other participants could actually recognise what they were meant to be! The hard part wasn't the painting, it was the drying. The teacher had provided paper-plates, folded into hacky holders for the candles. I hadn't accounted for the piece of candle around where it was held. So this would get smudged by the holder and ruin my mouse. After 3 redraws I just held the candle up in my hand. To dry it faster I decided I realised I could blow on the candle. I didn't want everyone else at the table to think I was a weirdo, well, at least not a weirdo that blows on candles for no reason. Therefore I decided to appeal to the authority of the teacher. I'd ask her about it, and when she confirmed blowing would speed up the drying process, I would blow.

"Ms Teacher. If we blow on the candles, will they dry faster?"

A long pause whilst she deliberates the question in her mind, cogs whirring, you can see her thinking hard.

"......*No. It won't*....Errrrrrr…Ok. That wasn't the answer I was hoping for. Don't want to be too up myself, but I'm fairly confident I'm correct here. Think of how sweat or clothes dry faster when cycling because of the breeze you build up. The moist air is taken away from just above the wet thing, so the moisture gradient between wet thing and air stays high, meaning it dries quicker right? Physics innit? So I just ignored her and started blowing.

The class came to a close, everyone inspected their handiwork and the others. We all pretended that each others were good and not dog dirt that belonged in the bin on the way out. I hadn't eaten on the ferry because the prices were eye-gouging. And hadn't had time before candling. So I was pretty famished. Food was priority. Man City supporter recommend Boojum (burritos), which also got Gary's seal of approval. But there's Boojum's in all big Irish cities, so I might as well try unique Dublin experiences whilst passing through.

Gary had recommended a couple of places. Felt I should trust the native Dublinite and go check them out. The first one I went to was Grogan's. Apparently has the best Guinness and out-of-this-world cheese toasties. I guess the rest of Dublin agreed with her, because it was absolutely flipping rammed. Sardines. Couldn't move without bumping into someone. Too much noise. Too claustrophobic. I couldn't be dealing with that. So I went looking for the #2 Guinness recommendation. The Gravediggers pub. This is all the way on the outskirts of Dublin, some 40 minutes walk away. But it seemed a nice walk along canals. Yes I know I've got a bike, but I'd locked it up in the hostel by this point, and it would have been a faff getting it out again. The Gravediggers was.......also rammed! Coming all this way, I ordered a Guinness anyway. As I'm ordering it, I notice a sign saying: **"customers MUST be wearing smart attire"**. I'm in my Adidas trackies, with duct-taped, beat-up Adidas trainers; like some budget Stormzy. Feeling self-conscious I put on some weird posh British accent to cover for the classlessness of my clothes. As I'm getting my pint the guy ordering next to me angrily pipes up: "*This wouldn't have stood in the old days*". Fuck. I tense up. Is he talking about an Englishman, a posh Englishman, getting a pint in this old Irish pub...or a scruffy scrote in Adidas getting one? I'm priming myself for a confrontation. i.e. How fast can I duck, weave and scamper out of here? But then he follows with "*Have ye not got time to let it settle?*"...Phew. He was only just aggrieved that the barman didn't serve the Guinness "properly": Pour most of it, let it settle, then top it off.

I took my Guinness, sat and drunk it on the kerb outside: Classy. Saturday probably isn't the best night for solo'ing around Dublin. It feels like literally the whole city is out on the piss, plus thousands of stumbling tourists. Always feels like you're in the way. Despite the Guinness not being settled, it was still the nicest Guinness I've ever had...although if I were to describe it, it would just be Guinness but slightly watered down. So I am almost certainly not a good judge of Guinness. Should probably get someone who actively likes Guinness for that.

Another 40 minute stroll back into central Dublin. Eyes eagerly scanning for good places to eat...scratch that, places to eat! An audible chuckle walking past a restaurant named "**4-Star Pizza**". They could have called their restaurant literally anything. Nothing stopped them from calling it 5-star...but you've got to appreciate their integrity and honesty. Nope. We're a 4-star pizza place, that's what we are, so that's gonna be our name! Certainly makes a refreshing change from the British kebab shops which always ave ridiculous names such as: "**Kebab King**", "**Best Kebab #1**" (Almost always found in a small village, where they are the *ONLY* kebab shop. Congrats. You've won by default.), "**Sell your Firstborn to buy Kebab and your life will have no regrets!**". Without fail they are always "just alright". I've never had a kebab that changed my life. I've had a kebab that forced me to change my sheets, although the quaddie-voddies should probably take some of the blame there. Oh, Dublin did also have a place called "**Kebabish**". It's Kebab….ish xD

I eventually stumbled across a "**Bunsen Burger**", another Gary tip. Actually a terrible tip for a failing vegetarian…or a very good tip if we're emphasising the failing. Because after not having eaten since breakfast, and it being nearly 8pm, and being denied food at the two establishments I trekked to…I caved. I caved hard. The cool thing about Bunsen Burger is their menu is on tiny business cards, and is just "burger", "burger with cheese". So I got a big burger and it was flipping delicious. I am jealous of the vegetarians who actually don't enjoy the texture or taste of meat.

Next stop: The Liberties. A hip and trendy part of Dublin, away from the rowdy Temple Bar. Recommended to me after asking: "Where do the floppy-fringe hipster kids hang out?"

I went to a bar called Lucky Something, maybe just Luckies. Another Guiness. Overwhelmingly busy again. Expected by this point. Resigned to this being the Dublin Saturday night experience. I squeezed into a tiny free spot on a bench by the outdoor pizza place. The music this evening was jazz. Ewww. Jazz jazz as well. Some jazz can be alright, but to me, 95% of jazz-jazz makes me feel no emotions, yet it also does not make me want to boogie my body. So then what the flip is it doing? All it accomplishes is demonstrating how talented the musicians playing it must be. Like the Beckham, Gerrard, Lampard era of England. Insanely talented individuals. Dire results.

I hadn't had pudding, so the highlight of Luckies was a flipping massive wood-fired garlic pizza bread. Only a few euros. Great bargain. You could really taste the wood. Very garlicky. Also unwittingly unearthing the ultimate cold-opener chat-up line…

Sick of the jazz I wandered on. Made for Whelan's, small indie-band venue. I turn up at the doors, two bouncers. One guy dealing with another bag. The other door-woman a sour face, looked at me like dog dirt on her shoe. Pure contempt.

Quel surprise, tickets for the small indie band I'd planned on seeing had sold out. No I couldn't just pop into the downstairs bar for a drink whilst I work out alternatives. So I popped into the first pub across the street. Thankfully no moody doormen...door-people...to bar my entry. Ordered myself a local IPA, done with Guinness. Yes the Guinness in Ireland tastes better...but it's still just Guinness. Sat on the bar-stools to avoid taking up a table. Next to a good looking, mediterannean-ish, youngish (somewhere between the age of 25 and 50...I'm flipping terrible with ages) woman. She was on her own nursing a pint. Had her phone out, with a big piece of supermarket chocolate cake in a plastic tray next to it.

Minded my own business for a while, trying and failing to write some bits of novel. But kept getting distracted, as she seemed fairly bored out of my peripheral vision. I wanted to be a bit more proactive with meeting women this trip. So what's the worst that could happen from saying hi?

This is where the garlic bread comes in: "*Hey, I'm <blank>. You should know, I've just eaten a massive amount of garlic bread. So if my breath is overwhelming, just let me know and I'll direct my mouth in the other direction*".

She didn't seem to mind, claiming I wasn't too garlicky. Just the right level of garlic. Bullshit. That was so much garloc (**editor note**: Garlock sounds like a an evil spellcaster who draws his power from the mighty garlic). In hindsight, the genius in the garlic line lies in how polite people can respond to it. The problem with nice people, fucking dicheads them nice folks…the problem with nice people, is that even if you say "*Look, if I'm boring you, just tell me to feck off. I don't mind*"; many still feel uncomfortable doing that. Instead, I'm 20 minutes into a monologue on magic mushrooms, whilst their subtle hints fly right over my head, ruining their evening. For me, the failure to notice hints and move on, is a bigger deterrent than rejection. So with the garlicky breath, it gifts the nice person an out. Something they can latch onto and say "please bring this interaction to a halt", without feeling too rude. Also, if they pretend it's fine, and are willing to endure the fumes; then you know they must be somewhat into you. Or maybe they just garlick (**editor note**: "*Or maybe they just garlic?*" Are you garlic this evening? Why yes, I am garlic as a matter of fact. Are you garlic?). In which case we already have something in common.

So anyway, we chatted for a bit. Coincidentally, she was actually working in Whelan's and was on a break. Offered to sneak me in to see the band. I told her I appreciated the offer, but then I opened my rucksack and showed her what was inside: "*Yeah. You're Fucked!*" I'd picked up supplies for the Galway ride right before popping in here. My bag contained hundreds of biscuits and an obscene amount of fluids. There was no-way the door-people were gonna allow this. Eventually she had to get back for her second shift half, then I drifted around like a bum. Strolled through Temple Bar, people-watching the drunken louts, pretending I'm Louis Theroux. Got an ice-cream. Nearly slipped in a disturbingly large pool of blood. Standard Dublin night out things. Made my way back to the hostel. Shit sleep again…when will I learn?

Ireland Day 2: Galloping to Galway. Wind Up My Bum.

I flipping hate hostels. I was woken around 5am by someone getting up. I don't mind that...but then when it's my turn to get up...I feel so bad. I was up at 7am. Every movement I made seemed to be hundreds of decibels. As I would try to stuff things into my bag, they'd inevitably spill out, and loudly roll across the floor. I ended up dragging all my clothes down to the reception bit. Getting dressed into my cycling gear in the toilets. It's silly, if I don't mind, then I shouldn't feel so guilty when I make noise. Alas it doesn't seem to follow logic.

With the Anglesey struggles, I'd not fully committed to riding all the way to Galway. There was no solid plan. If I'd have been on one the night before, the tea-acceptance timeline, then I may have been in no fit state to ride. Even without a big one, the weather forecast had looked pretty grim. Rain, rain, rain.

On the morning itself I was tired but not hungover. The forecast was better, still rain, but not all day. The most important thing was it wasn't raining for my departure. Once you're into the ride, and your body temps are up, the rain can feel refreshing. It's mainly starting in rain which is cold and depressing. Bonus: a pretty big tailwind. With everything looking up, I got my gear on, and set off as it was getting light. Can always bail and train the second half.

The morning started with a ride through the sleepy, hungover Dublin city. Onto Phoenix Park: A big green space on the Eastern edge of Dublin. Lots of grass with a big penisy monument. You might recognise it from the Youtube Matt Stephens cafe ride with David O Doherty. I did not go Full David and go over the handlebars clowning around. Unfortunately I saw no deer.

I really should have taken the train. Man the countryside in central Ireland is mediocre. It's not "bad", but it's not much different to the UK countryside. Similar to the Anglesey ride, it might have been nicer if I went off the semi-main roads and through the villages, but I didn't really have the time to do that. On my cycle computer, a little screen attached to my bikes handlebars, it shows "distance to next turning". This is a nice way of "chunking" big rides, so you can focus on just getting to the next turning, and not the extra 100 miles you've got to do after that…but this route was incredibly direct. Each time I got to a roundabout it was:

"Next turning: 8miles"...roundabout..."Next turning: 14 miles"..."Next turning: 23 miles". There were nice bits, but overall it was a dull route and a "get it done" type day.

I was also fortunate to meet a nice, friendly chap called Colm, who kept me company for one of the long 14mile stretches. Colm had been out riding with his local club, but recovering from a cold had turned back home, and came across me. An ex-racer, he was dead keen on cycling. Showered me with tips and places for Irish cycles. This trip I wouldn't take him up on his "*Fuck Limerick. Go Killarney*" suggestion, but it's on my "TODO" list for next year. I was taken aback by how much he seemed to care about the weather and rain. This became a common theme across my trip. I'd have thought that with so much rain, the people of Ireland would just get on with it. They'd be used to it, immune. But no, it was always something worth commenting on, and something to base your plans around. However I did appreciate Colm's quote, maybe a common saying, but I heard it from him: "*Ireland would be the perfect country; if only it had a roof*".

He had seemed very impressed at me keeping pace with him whilst riding San, in battered adidas trainers. We all like to pretend we limit our ego. But I feel like everyone still gets a warm, pleasant sensation from other people thinking they're good at things. I reckon even Buddhist monks are secretly really egotistical about how unegotistical they are.

I know I just commented on Irish people not shutting up about the weather....but the weather...I got so lucky on this cross-country ride. There were dark clouds all around, yet somehow the rain held and held, like well trained archers. It briefly spattered a bit in the late afternoon, but that was it. And the wind. God damn. Colm said the prevailing wind was usually West to East. If that had been the case today, I'm almost certain I would have given up and got the train. But this significant East-to-Westerly made it do-able. It's not just the change in physical exertion. The mental side of feeling like the Earth and the elements are not working against you, but on your side and willing you forwards. Very motivating.

Stopped at my first Supermacs and got a veggie burger. Interesting. Not going for the fake-meat style. Grew on me with every bite. Ate a lot of food. Drank a lot of drink. Looked at a lot of cows. Got looked at by a lot of cows. Very curious animals. Felt guilty about the delicious bunsen burger I'd had the day before. I'm sorry I ate you Mr Cow :(

Roughly half-way across the country I stumbled across a town called Ballinasloe. The whole place was fenced off for something. Forcing me off my bike and hiking. I saw a horse. Then a pony. Then another horse. On about the fifth horse I gathered that it was a horse festival. The young women at this horse festival were….something else. I don't like negatively commenting on peoples appearances, but I can't just ignore what I witnessed. This was...surreal. Half of the young women looked like totally normal Irish women. But the other 50% were dressed to drag-queen levels. Swanky cocktail dresses, massive heels, a dump-truck of makeup, enough spray-tan to get themselves pulled from netflix. Like Made-in-Essex turned up to 11. I wasn't sure what to do with my eyes. Like when you see someone with a noticeable deformity, and you don't want to stare, but you also don't want to avoid looking, so you look "a normal amount"....but then what's normal. It was absurd watching these women in high-end dresses and shoes, literally wading through streets of horse shite. Strangest experience of the trip. Upon returning, a quick google suggested part of the festival is a beauty pageant, which is a semi-explanation. It does not fully explain their Donald-Trump-esque definition of "beauty".

The further West I went, the windier the wind got. Getting really fun after Ballinasloe. Barely tapping the pedals. Sights improving too. You probably have a mental picture of rural Ireland. Once you get into Galway county, you start to see it. The myriad of low stone-walls surrounding green sheep-fields.

I could start to see great looming shapes on the horizon. Jeez. I was hoping these weren't hills I would have to cross to get into Galway, big! After checking the map and seeing how close I was, these must be the Aran Islands in the distance (note: I later found out this shape was the Burren, big hills on the other side of Galway bay...not the Aran Islands at all). Wow, the Aran Islands looked so impressive (note: again. Not the Aran Islands. But I thought they were at this stage). Eventually I reached Oranmore, where you're treated to your first sight of the Atlantic. With the Burren on the horizon and a beautiful rainbow appearing as I stopped...It felt truly magical. Otherworldly. I'm so glad I didn't just take the train. Not only would you miss this view and moment. You miss the multiplying effect of the rewarding aspect of having earnt this moment. It's a bit like how you can just have a Hot Chocolate at any time....but a Hot Chocolate after you've been out hiking all day, you've just put your wet socks on the radiator, sat down in front of a cozy fire...that Hot Chocolate tastes 100 times better.

Cruising into Galway the tailwinds were literally getting up to nearly 40mph. Mental. It genuinely felt like the universe was lifting me up and carrying me to Galway. In the morning I'd informed my host that I almost certainly wouldn't arrive until 7, therefore she had loads of time to get the room ready. Thanks to the wind I was literally in Galway by 5pm. A bicycle tour of the charming city whilst I waited. A street market led to a big pancake, followed up with a humongous loaf of focaccia bread. Glorious carbs. Glorious glycogen. Cracking cathedral. The place had a lovely vibe. Still lots of tourists, but less "night-out" tourists. Sprinkle in many students as well. The tourists and students give the city a really lively and optimistic vibe, which you can feel walking around.

Eventually I headed over to the house I'm staying in...technically it was booking.com, but it was just a spare room in someone's house, airbnb style. Into the outskirts and up a steep hill to get to it, I pull up at number 13, my lucky number (I was born on Friday the 13th. There's something fun and counter-culture about taking an unlucky number as your lucky one). Maybe from the tone of the messages, really nice and friendly, but I was expecting a frail, old lady. So it was a bit of a shock when the front door opened. The smell of incense intoxicating and the host was breathtaking. Dreadlocks down to her feet. Like the predator from Predator; a sexy Predator. Cool headband and spiral earrings. Exotic voice, sort of Irish, sort of not. I was struggling with words a tad as I tried to answer her questions, e.g. did I want to lock the bike to her gate: "*Sorry if I'm slow. Words are hard now. Cycle big way*".

I'll give her the nickname Luna in this tale. I was a bit apprehensive about using the name of an actual Goddess. I'm not very religious, but why risk incurring wrath for no gain? I would have gone for Mirana, a priestess of the Moon. But I'd rather piss off the Gods than her. Also, Luna can be short for lunatic. Which you may also come to realise she is, I mean that in genuinely the best way possible! Maybe that's where the etymology of the word comes from? I wonder.

After finally working out the lock, bending over to give Luna a top view of my prime cycling muscles, I unpacked and had a chilled evening finishing my focaccia. Way too tired to trundle all the way back into central Galway and pub it up. I was there for multiple nights so there was no rush. I could also use the time to plan my next days. One of the main attractions around Galway are the Aran Islands. Very famous, not trying to make you feel bad if you haven't heard of them....I'd heard of them before planning Ireland trip, but thought they were Scottish for some reason. The Banshees of Inisheerin is loosely set on a "fictitious" Aran Island....but also did film quite a bit on Inish Mor (so is it really fictitious?). There's Inish Mor and two other Inishes, Inish Less? Doesn't matter, I was only going to the big daddy, Inish Mor. Ferry booked and I'd be up early tomorrow.

Incredible Ireland: Day 3. How I love thee. Mr Aran, Y U So Barren?

A personal blackout on Inish Mor photos and info ensured I'd maximise the wow factor today. I actually recommend you to skip the island part of this chapter and just go there. In the summer season there's a direct Galway ferry. In winter you have to go from Rossaveel. It's cyclable, and you can take your bike on the ferry, but the shuttle bus was cheap and I valued the extra sleep. It would be nice to have a days break from the bike. I also had a lurking feeling that it wasn't guaranteed to survive the adventure. No point adding unnecessary extra miles to it. San would be sitting this one out. Good job too.

Awake at 7am and getting ready. The room has a small kettle. I make myself a cup of tea. No milk sachets (Luna is vegan), so black it is.

I was leaving for the ferry at 8am. At 7:43am I brewed the cup of tea. At 7:44am I put the cup of tea on the ground whilst I pottered about. At 7:45am the cup of tea had been completely forgotten. As I walked over to the bedside table....**blinding pain**! No scream. The type of shocking pain that forces your eyebrows to the top of your head, and forces you to inhale deeply. Can't really scream whilst inhaling. I look down to see the mug sideways and my sock drenched. Initially I'm more concerned about staining the carpet and am running around with toilet roll. Then I remember that this is possibly the most intense pain I'd ever experienced? Short but sharp. Maybe my foot should take priority? I take the sock off and start running the foot under the cold shower. It no longer "hurts", but it definitely feels weird and the skin is sloughing off. The shower water pooling in the peeling skin forming a water balloon.

I have no idea how bad a burn this is. Certainly not trivial, but does it need the hospital? Don't want to be a drama queen. There's only one ferry to the Alan Islands a day. So it's hospital vs ferry. Which do I go for?

I leave the decision as late as possible, it's still hard to tell how bad the burn is. But I decide that if I start walking to the shuttle bus, if I do need a hospital, it might become clearer on the way.

So I whack some chunky plasters on it, put my normal shoe on my right foot, and put my "surfing/plimsol" type shoe on my left foot. Lucky I brought these, they're technically surfing shoes. I like them for cycling because they squish up as small as flip-flops, but feel more like proper shoes. The squishyness means they'll rub the burns less.

I pick up some specific burn plasters and burn gel from a pharmacy before the shuttle bus, just in-case I need them later. Then wait for my bus. Try not to think about the foot. It's 80% Americans in line for the bus. A friendly old couple, whose names I've unfortunately forgotten, chat in the line with me. The time passes quickly. On the bus to Rossaveel, then on the ferry. Before I know it we're in the Atlantic ocean and it's a bit late for the hospital.

My feet aren't hurting per se. But when nerve-endings can be burnt through...is that a good thing? It's more of a throbbing sensation, not really unpleasant, kind of interesting. I try to avoid looking at my foot. One glance down has demonstrated that my burn blisters have already swelled and filled with quite a lot of fluid. Again I have no idea how good/bad this is. Is this normal healing? I just try and get on with the day and hope I don't have to amputate it later.

Oh boy. This ferry. It had been a long time since I've been properly seasick. But this small boat was struggling in the Atlantic waves. Looking out the window it was sky, sea, sky, sea. Some serious tiltage, fairground-fide levels. For those worried about seasickness, the ferry is only 45 minutes, the choppiness seems confined to the open-water midsection, and you can stand out on top-deck. Hope it doesn't put people off, but maybe pack some motion sickness tablets.

Pulling up on Inish Mor, the sea is crystal clear. You can see tiny little fishes swimming around in it. We pulled into the little port. The ways to get around Inish Mor are cheap rented bicycles, free? minibuses, or horse and cart. Horse and cart sounds cool, but I like to be in charge of where I'm heading. I rented a bike nearby and set out towards the north of the island. I would recommend staying overnight on Inish Mor if you can. You can almost see the whole island by bike in a day trip. Almost. However, with only a single daily ferry home, you get a bit nervous about missing it and being stuck overnight. Most people head back to the porty bit in good time, mill around the pub and gift shops. Knowing there's no ferry to miss, you could explore the whole island with no time pressure.

I head straight for the seal colony. Not graceful creatures, but they have such cute faces. Definitely the doggos of the sea. I couldn't wait to see them up close. Now when I ask you to imagine a seal colony, and picture it in your head....how many seals do you have in your mind? Probably a lot right? Probably a lot more than six? Yeah, six. I was expecting a tad more than six grey, flubbery seals; lazing around on the high-tide shorline, doing literally nothing. Far enough that I have to squint at each one, carefully verifying if it is indeed a seal, or actually just a large rock. Hopefully the island gets better...

From the seals I biked to Dun Aengus. Inish Mor is the most wonderful place I've been. It's hard to justify. Initially I'd put most beautiful. That's incorrect. Ot is the most wonderful. It's certainly less spectacular than the Alps, or other mountainous places....but there's something about it. A beauty in spite of how barren and exposed it is. And the sound. There's nothing but the menacing "dumph"ing of waves into the cliffs, the whistling of the wind, the caws of the gulls, and the "oh geez" of the flocks of american tourists, struggling with the most rudimentary stone steps up to Dun Aengus. Poor guys. Clinging onto the wire fence for dear life.These people would not have made it up Snowdon. Although I shouldn't be too harsh, the clambering over rocks isn't advertised as part of visiting Aran. Reaching Dun Aengus offers stunning views, but is full of Americans: "Oh my Gawd!". Maybe another reason to overnight it. Imagine being there alone, on your own, as the sun sets. Right, I'm pretty sure I have to go back and do that now.

My favourite part came from deciding to branch off the main road, onto the far side of the island. Although isn't that the way with life in general? The road less travelled offers us the most unique and memorable experiences. Road is a generous word here. It became a jumble of rocks. The rental bike got absolutely battered. So glad I left San at home. Almost certain I'd trashed the bottom bracket or something by the time I dropped it off. Proper clonking sound going on. These rocky roads led from Dun Aengus to "The Wormhole". If you go to an island with something called "The Wormhole", how can you live with yourself if you don't see it?

Turns out the Wormhole wasn't anything special. I was not overwhelmed. Just a regular amount of whelmed. I'd got excited after the brochure FAQ had "Can I swim in the wormhole?" "No. It is too dangerous to swim in the wormhole"......yeah, its a bloody wormhole (still don't know what it means by wormhole yet...but that made it sound really badass). I don't know how to describe it really, google it or go there I guess? The route on foot to the wormhole was the actual highlight. It was over a kilometre of walking, across chunky natural stones and rocks. When you got to the coastal bit, you're sort of on a cliff, but there was also water and rock-pools everywhere. Maybe from high-tide, or maybe from the spray of the waves splashing? So the final stretch to the wormhole was full of shallow pools, mosses, mini-caves carved out of the imposing rock. It looked like a different world. A world out of Dune or Star Trek. Birthtaking!

Rode around some more, trashed the bike some more. The rocks chunkier and chunkier. I'd recommend an electric bike by the way. Even I, the cycling monster, got off and walked up some bits of the island. A cardinal sin in cycling. Fortunately there was literally no-one to witness this embarrassment. I loved the freedom and the remoteness of the far side of the island. You could get your willy out anywhere (or your vag).

Skipping across more stones towards Dún Dúchathair (Black fort), I did nearly stack it a couple of times, rolling my ankle on the rocks. It made me think….if you're alone, and you break your ankle out here...it could genuinely be a loooong time before anyone finds you. Tried to be a wee bit more careful after that. Even finally tucked my nob back in.

There's a Sea Power album (they're a band) called Man of Aran. They wrote an alternative soundtrack to a really old documentary on the Aran islands. Great piece of music and really fits with the place. So I was cruising round listening to that. Pausing now and again to just experience the ras audio of the island. Gobsmacked is the correct word. Just shaking my head at how amazing the place was. Verge of tears. How lucky I was that I can visit places like this, and that I'm healthy enough to buzz around on a bike (ignoring the heavily burnt foot). I love you Alan.

Meandered my way back to the port in good time for the ferry. A sturdy pub lunch and some souvenirs. Typical tourist stuff.

I cannot recommend Inish Mor more highly, and I'll certainly be back to see the other two islands and complete the set, probably next year.

Whilst I'd been heading to the island, Luna (my host) had messaged me. She was busy during the day, off at a photo-shoot. But in the evening she was going to a Ceilidh class and did I want to tag along? I had no idea what a Ceilidh was. Apparently it was going to be about 2 hours of learning some Irish set dancing, then everyone headed to a pub afterwards where they were doing a music session, and we'd do drinks and dancing there.

I was slightly apprehensive. Mainly because of the foot. I've literally never done any form of organised dancing. And if someone ending up stomping on my fluid-filled foot….that was going to be messy. But when a literal (part-time) model invites you to go dancing then drinking with her…..you'd have to amputate to stop me saying yes to that.

So a ferry and a bus back to Galway, and the class was just round the corner. I nervously went in the pub and walked through to the back-room where the class would be. Luna was there chatting to a friend, looking unreal in a beautiful black dress and flowing hair. I met Joe the head-honcho. A smart-looking young guy with a well trimmed beard. At ceilidh classes each dance consists of a sequence of "moves", and the instructor will call out the next move like "house", "spin" or "advance and retreat". That was Joe's job, as well as providing demonstrations and help where needed. Being a beginner class, a lot was needed!

People filtered into the mediumly sized room. Not massive, not cramped. The kind of room where small, local gigs happen. Capacity in the low hundreds, if that. We warmed up with a tappy foot pattern Joe wanted us to learn. Sounds so simple but surprisingly difficult to execute. We took randomish partners and dived straight into the first sets. Starting out simple. e.g. 4 people in a line holding hands step towards another 4 in time to the music. Then retreat. Then you join hands with your partner opposite you. Do a bit of skipping around, a bit of spinning. It was pretty fun and not too hard to pickup if you have rhythm.

We switched to a different song and I was dancing with Luna as my partner. She was leader and me follower as a newbie. As we linked hands and placed arms around each others waist and shoulders I could feel my cock twitch excitedly (**editor note**: that feels a bit too much information...but I want a realistic account. And if I have a throbbing semi. Then that's what goes in the book. Sorry mum). So now I had to contend with avoiding both my foot blister exploding, and getting a massive bonk-on in tracksuit trousers that do not conceal well. But as the music got going I could focus on that and get lost in it. I was picking it up really well, Luna and I both laughing when I did cock up. Most of the moves were alright, it was just "House" that caused my brain to go into catastrophic meltdown, my feet to suddenly move according to a random number generator. To this day if you want to see my panic-face, just sneak up behind me and whisper "House" in my ear. We tried to practice it between songs, but even that didn't help much. "House is actually fairly simple. It's basically just a waltz."......well I *basically* don't know how to fucking waltz do I? So that helps me how?

House-panic aside, the class was class. Everyone worked up a massive sweat. A lot more fun than running on a treadmill for two hours. After class we popped to an oldy pub down the street, where a trad-music session was in progress. Joe had a word with the players, and they agreed to play a few ceilidh-able tunes. One song was simple enough for me to join in. Very surreal, having only done it for 2 hours, now dancing in a pub to an Irish music session, whilst American tourists whipped out their cameras amazed. The dances got a bit more complex, a bit faster, so I just sat back, enjoyed watching, chatted with people from the class. There was a good mix, some older people. Many young studenty people. Luna was driving so I didn't force her to hang around too long (I think. Hard to tell when I'm drinking and having a good time. Time melts.). We drove back, talked about anything and everything. About both living in Sweden for 6 months during the winter and how miserable that was. Talked about mushrooms, her shaman practices. This and that. Felt really comfortable and natural. She was different enough from me to be an incredibly interesting person, but also felt like a kindred spirit in many ways.

Incredible Ireland: Day 4. Gimme More

What a day 1 in Galway it had been. Galway day 2 was more cycling. I had the club challenge of my monthly 200km ride I wanted to get done. So I set off early. My goal: Sky road to the Northwest on the coast near Clifton. I hadn't looked at any pics to avoid spoiling myself, but "Sky Road" just sounded like a place that had to have top notch views. The route there could also follow the famous "Wild Atlantic Way", quickly becoming a must-see route for cyclists. I left Galway going north, planning to cycle through the funny named Upper Cloosh and Maam Cross towards Clifton. However, as I got onto the main road Clooshbound, it was obnoxiously busy with cars. The cycle computer said: "*35 miles until next turning*". You fuckin wot m8?! No thanks. So I cut back and went down the road following the coast instead. Still a bit busy, especially with people trying to get to the morning ferry in Rossaveel. But nicer sights, and not busy for too long. In hindsight I think if you follow Wild Atlantic Way signs out of Galway, there might be a route avoiding both of these busy roads. But I didn't want to fuss about replanning routes.

Stopped in An Spideal (Irish for The Spider) for an early coffee and cakes. There was a little window bakery there, I got a cookie as a tester. So impressed I stocked up on energy balls, croissants, flapjack, all the good stuff. I'd stopped as I was not feeling energetic and needed the caffeine. In hindsight and looking at the map, this place is right outside of Galway....I must have been so drained at this point in the trip. Stopping 10% of the way into a ride is unheard of for me. Dublin to Galway, then straight into Aran Islands, with a messed up foot, followed by hours of dancing and drinking. These must have been taking their toll.

As I reached Rossaveel the route peeled off and inland. Oh boy. These Wild Atlantic Roads are right to be hyped. They are Wild. They are Atlantic. They are roads. Maybe it's fear of heights, but I preferred the views like these to mountain descents. The roads going North had an astoundingly barren landscape. Hardly any trees. Vast vistas stretching off to the horizon, silhouetted with mountains. The route was punctuated with little lakes or sea inlets, rocky formations; contrasting the stark emptiness. I followed these roads for ages. Seeing very little civilization. Mildly concerning. I had packed little food and water. If San broke here, it was going to be a very, very long walk.

But San kept going, held up just fine. I'm so used to riding San that by this point, it feels weird mentioning how surprised I am the bike is still going, or how much I'm enjoying riding it. We are becoming like a long time married couple. We don't need to tell each other every day. The love is implied. It's just normal. Maybe it shouldn't be implied? Maybe you should tell your partner you love them a bit more. Give their drivetrain a good lubing.

My body wasn't doing as well as San. Very tired. Coming back late and drunk, I'd let myself have a little lie-in and left late. Combined with the long stop in An Spideal, and it was already nearly 3pm. I hadn't even reached the half-way point and Sky Road. Flip. I was going to get back so late! But this is why we always bring our bike lights! I pushed on towards Clifton, no stops; no time. I was feeling that Clifton should be much closer, when finally I saw the sign for it, a little relief. I bought an expensive lunch in Clifton. Sandwich and crisps and a coke. Absolutely smashed it into my face-hole, way too fast to enjoy. Blitzkrieg lunch. But I needed to make up time.

Coming out of Clifton it immediately starts to climb. It's not a massive, massive hill. But still one of the biggest I'd done on the trip so far. Even before the true top, you go over a mini-crest and the view of the Atlantic opens up to you. The view I saw is now my phone wallpaper.

What a view. And the view galvanises you to push a bit further to the top. As you get to the top, you come around the side of the hill and back inland. Sky road is on a "spur", slightly sticking out into the Atlantic. More amazing views as you head back inland. Mountains in the distance, lakes/inlets in the foreground. Green and grey. Sheep and cute houses. Winding roads.

Passing back through Clifton it was pretty much the route out but in reverse. This sounds very boring, but it's kind of interesting to see the same place from a different angle. Also, recognising sights can really help with morale. Makes it feel like you can't be that far from home. This turned out to be pretty important. I was gassed. I'd been avoiding checking the mileage, eventually caved midway through the wildest part of the wilderness. I'd expected to see at least 100 miles, leaving maybe 30 left. But it was 80 miles, might even have been below. I just remember thinking: "Welp. This is gonna be a long day". But I did the thing I always do in these situations. Don't let yourself succumb to breaks every 5 minutes. Keep plodding along. Keep the wheels turning. Keep stuffing the bag of dry crackers into my face. And eventually I did reach a kind of hypnotic state. Where the extreme fatigue relaxes me and turns everything slightly absurd, like shifting TV contrast or colours to the max. In this surreal state I start to stomp on the pedals, faster and faster. The food I'd been chomping seemed like it'd replenish my stores a bit. I'd dug down and found more energy than I expected. A bit too out of it to appreciate the scenery in reverse, but made cracking progress. Powering through each lump and bump, of which there were a lot. It was less noticeable when leaving the house fresh, but the coast road back into Galway had no flat. Just bumpety, bumpety, bumpety. You bollock it up a mini-rise, semi-coast the other side. Bollock-it. Semi-coast. I eventually made it back into the beachey Salthill, then central Galway just as the sun was setting. I'd smashed the 2nd half.

Back in Galway the priority was food. **Boojum**: a burrito chain recommended highly by Gary and the candle-painting-Man-City-fan. I'd even noticed people wearing "*Boojum addict*" t-shirts. It was an institution here. After going veg, burrito has become my go-to "fast-food" in Canterbury. Enough vegetables that your brain deems it "healthy", but so chock full of rice and bread that it really replenishes your stores after a big day. I'm a spice-lover. The spices in other European countries seem a bit tame compared to Britain. Especially Netherlands, their 3-chill menu options make an embarrassment of their nation. So obviously here I went for the 4-chilli mega-hot naga sauce. How hot could it be? Holy macaroni! Phwoar! This was not to be trifled with. Blew the absolute fuck out of my mouth. It was the dangerous kind of spice, where it doesn't seem too hot on first bite. But as you go through the meal, the heat just builds and builds and builds. To a thundering crescendo of fire and brimstone. Nose is streaming, mucus dripping back into what still remains. But you cannot admit defeat; especially after attacking the meal with such outrageous hubris. You yell in your brain "C'MON! I CAN DO IT!". Roar under your breath with each bite, as you battle your way through the end.

I really need to go back to Boojum. Because I literally have no idea what their burritos taste like. Other than overconfidence and regret. Mouth still burning, I ran to the nearest ice-cream shop. Feels good man. Back at the gaff I was so knackered I wasn't going to hit the town a 2nd night in a row. Luna was out for some friends thing anyway, so nothing to tempt me out of the comfy, warm bed.

Incredible Ireland: Day 5. Revive and Energize

There were more epic cycles I wanted to do out from Galway. Explore more of the twisting, winding coastline of Connemara. Explore the great lakes. I'd been concerned about San, but it was my body telling me it was at breaking point. My knee hadn't been in proper pain the day before. But I'd noticed the ache rising, and had started concentrating on flaring my hips a bit wider, turning my left foot inwards. Reducing the lateral forces going through my knee. If I bashed out another 100-miler today, either the knee would go, or my overworked body would succumb to a cold. Intuition told me this wasn't a day to be ignoring my body's signals. So the itinerary was a casual ride around Galway. See the city. Soak in the sunshine. Become a regular tourist for the day.

In the morning Luna had offered to take me sea-swimming in the evening. Is saltwater good for a badly burnt foot?. I didn't even google it. Not going to pass up this opportunity. If you'd have told me Galway had shark-infested waters, if Luna had dived in, I would follow. The weather was now early October and bitingly cold. Summer was over. I had no proper swimming gear, just my underpants. Hopefully she knew about shrinkage.

I'd had so much fun at the Ceilidh, and now sea-swimming. I'd never met a holiday host like Luna. Someone who went to such considerable lengths to make her guests stays in Galway as memorable and magical as possible. There was no question, I had to buy a present to show even a sliver of the gratitude I felt. This became my mission for the day. My mind went back to when she first opened the door, the heavy waft of incense hitting me. That seemed like a good simple gift. Incense. My other consideration was whiskey from the local distillery, but I didn't know if she even liked whiskey. Plus I already felt like getting a present and card might be a bit odd, didn't want to go too expensive and make it too weird. Thoughtful, but within budget. That's my approach to romance.

So I typed "incense" into google maps, and one of the two red blobs was actually in the Menlow area where I would be cycling. A bit surprising, that area didn't look very "shoppy", but why not swing by. So after a chilled lie-in off I set. In the lovely sunshine, once again absolutely blessed by the weather in Galway. Menlow area was cosy suburbs?

Suburbs is the wrong word, it makes you think of modern, identical rows of houses. This was predominantly charming older housing. Overgrown gardens, birds singing. I stopped by the edge of the lake, a family feeding the ducks. Really calm and idyllic place. I reached where Google Maps claimed the shop was. "Shop". As it said "*destination arrived*" I searched with my eyes. My special eyes.....where? Where is this "shop"? The only thing I noticed was several black cats prowling around, very odd. I asked the cats about the shop. They were incredibly unhelpful. In the cat's garden there was a tiny shed, a Portakabin. I went over to it and had a nose in the window. Candles, boxes. No life. Knocked on the door. Nothing. I was just about to leave when a stout oldish, splotchy-faced man trundled over from the house. "*Hello*"

"Hi, I errr...wanted to buy some incense and it said on the internet there was a shop here?"

"*What?*"

"Incense. Do you sell incense? This is the candle place right?"

"*Yeah I make candles in the shed here. Where did you see the stuff?.....online....my son handles the online stuff. Me and technology don't see eye-to-eye*"

He welcomed me into the shed where he made all the candles.

"So you don't do incense?"

"*No, I just make candles*"

"Look, on the webstore it has boxes of incense. Have you stopped doing them?"

"*Ahhh, we had a terrible fire out back the other week. So all we've got is what's in here*"

So it was clear they didn't have incense. Before I could leave he launched into a 15 monologue on the candles, punctuated only by my occasional "hmmm". Apparently he and his son had been making candles for many years. They specialised in decorative candles, e.g. christenings, or remembering loved ones. He had **revolutionised** the field of decorative candles. The problem with a memorial candle is...when you burn it, the memorial melts away. Maybe this should be a metaphor on the ephemerality of life, and how everyone fades from memory eventually. But candle-man didn't see it that way, and saw it as a problem to be solved. He had revolutionised them, by hollowing them out, and placing bottles of oil inside them. Which meant the oil burnt, but not the candle. So the candle would live forever, and you just had to keep changing the oil. I didn't ask if one of these led to the terrible fire.

Eventually I piped up that I better be off. He proudly gave me a brand new red candle for free. I don't want to be ungrateful. But it's 2024. What the fuck am I going to do with one candle in 2024? Let alone three*! Not even enough to make an overused pun. It was still a heart-warming gesture. I'm very grateful for the thought behind it though, so I plopped it in my bag as I rolled back off into town.

*Including the two Dublin-paintings.

Bee-lined to a slightly more sensible shop that sold incense. One of the lovely-smelling, hippie type shops like Siesta in Canterbury. I picked up some incense that reminded me of the scent of her house. With a chill day to kill I just wandered round the shop, soaking up the ambience; the strangeness of the merchandise. I selected a card with a forest scene which seemed to suit Luna. Then a small piece of jet black Obsidian, which made me think of her. Matched her hair. Matched her soul. Importantly it was small enough to not be a: "*and where the fuck do I put this?*" nuisance kind of gift. What are the best kind of gifts? Small and easily recyclable! Then I saw something and fell in love. A jumble of cool, colourful lizards. Each about the length of a forearm, filled with sand. Some bright rainbow colours, others more realistic. All with cute red felt tongue poking out. When I picked it up it was super weighty. I thought "*no way I can carry this on the bike through Wicklow mountains*"; reluctantly placed it back in the basket. I went to leave. My feet were rooted to the spot. The more I thought about it, the more it made sense. Something about the absurdity of cyclists going to inordinate lengths shaving a few grams off their setup….and I'm buying a gigantic fucking sand-filled lizard to place in my panniers. In an absurd universe, sometimes insanity is the only logical choice. When the going gets weird: The weird turn pro! The idea was too comical. So I bought it. Back home he now lives on my fridge, he's one of the realistic looking ones, mottled greens. I occasionally pick him up and lie down with him on my chest. He's roughly the same weight as a small cat. Reminds me of our old family cats, the pleasant weightiness of them lying on your chest. Aaahhh.

So I paid for Mr Lizard, incense, card and stone. Spent the next few hours loitering around town. Being a menace.

Bothering coffee shop employees about music (Cranberries, Stone Roses, Smiths, The Cure etc were on the playlist). Bothering them about Charleoi. The worst place I've ever had the misfortune of cycling through. Bought some food gifts for people back home. 66% of these did not survive the journey un-nibbled...but it's the thought that counts.

Eventually I worked my way back to the house. If things went to plan, It was my last night in Galway. I'd be setting off and ending up in Limerick tomorrow evening. I partially packed, then messaged Luna letting her know I was "ready" for sea-swimming. Luna drove us down to Blackrock, on the edge of Galway. Named because the rocks are….well you can guess. Stone/paving juts out into the sea, steps leading down to the splashing waves on either side. Culminating in a large 5-ish meter diving tower. In the distance on the far side of the bay you see the domineering shapes of The Burren. To your right you see patches of dark sand, a red sunset attempting to break through the clouds. Luna pops into the rudimentary stone changing rooms, gets changed and sorts her hair out.

She can't let her dreadlocks get wet, at least not in the evening when they won't have time to dry. So she had to tie them up and claimed she'd look like Marge Simpson. As she emerged from the changing rooms I was slightly disappointed. Her hair was folded on top of each other like a pastry, and reached barely even 40% Marge Simpson height. There were maybe 20 other locals around, most out of water, hanging around, chatting. Seems people would hop in for a bit, then hop out. It's not like your local pool where people will do laps for an hour. I'd kept all my clothes on until the last possible minute. Then frantically declothed down to just my boxers.

A seasoned sea swimmer (literally: she still dives in in December), Luna informed me: "*It shouldn't be too cold. You'll be fine. You won't die*". Oh. Good. Then proceeds to immediately pull a pair of fancy swimming gloves and shoes out of her bag. "*Oh, these are just so my fingers or toes don't fall off*".....right. No special shoes. No gloves. There's me standing there in just my boxers, already shivering. Luna finishes getting ready, walks to the steps, lowers herself in, lets out a few involuntary sounds indicating "It shouldn't be too cold" may have been bullshit. But then composes herself and begins gracefully and calmly breaststroking around. She beckons me to follow. I take a deep breath at the edge. Come on. I expect it's going to be cold. I step down the ladder. HO-LEE-FUCK. It's way colder than I even anticipate. Only my lower body is in, but I just commit. Remove the ability to wuss out and shamefully slink back up the ladder. As the rest of the body goes in, the shock increasing. My brain is scrambling around, not used to such intense sensations. My breathing wild. I push away from the ladder and then I'm treading water. The shock had hit me like a tonne of bricks. I'd told Luna that I wasn't a strong swimmer, but at least I'm not a drowner...yet the cold seemed to have incapacitated my muscles. It felt like it was taking everything to just keep myself afloat. I tried swimming around a bit but my arms had no power. The waves washed salty water down my throat as I was gulping for breath. Hopefully Luna found my panicked thrashing endearing, or at least amusing. I can't remember. I was focussed on not dying, one of my favourite hobbies. When it comes to seducing women, not drowning is highly recommended. As time went on I acclimatised more and more. Panicked less and less. Still couldn't really swim, but at least I didn't feel in mortal danger. I was actually surprised when Luna said: *"Alright, that's enough for me"* and headed out. Felt like I could stay in, but I don't fully understand hypothermia and it felt best to quit whilst ahead. Whilst I've been focussing on the panic, it's both panic and exhilarating. And then when you've calmed down, you've still got some of the exhilaration. Certainly makes you feel alive. If the criminal water companies didn't keep pumping raw sewage onto the Kent coastline, I would be doing this back home way more often. But anyway, not wanting to underestimate the effects of the cold, I followed Luna out.

Once out of the water, I had my sights on the tower. Surely I had to try a jump. I didn't even have to dive, just a regular jump. No skill required. Just the bravery. And was it even bravery? It just feels scary. "*I'm gonna jump*" I whispered to Luna. "*OK*" she chuckled. She got out her phone as I waddled over to the tower. Clambering up the steps I reached the top. Oh dear; that looks high. Standing at the edge and looking down it suddenly seems waaay higher than from the ground. I'd wanted to jump immediately, the longer you wait, the more the tension builds. But there was a small kid on the lower board, looking like he wanted to jump. He kept pussying out. What a pussyhole that small child was. Finally he turned back, slunk off in disgrace. Now it was my turn. Walked up to the edge. I can't do this can I? I never consciously chose to jump. Mr Lizard intervened. Fear of looking silly. How embarrassing would it be, to be no braver than a 7 year old child. Next thing I know I'm falling. The water rushes up to meet your feet. Panic. Adrenaline. I'm going to die! Plunge. Muffled sounds (dooosh). Sound coming back as you rise to the surface, legs flailing. Breathe uncontrollable, muscles confused. Claw your way back to shore. Wild grin, wild eyes. Whew!

In my head it had been a graceful, casual walk; then a spritely hop up and plunge down. Graceful. On rewatching

Luna's video, it looked more like an office-worker deciding he'd had enough, stepping off the edge to bring an end to it all.

Me and Luna hung around for a bit, pulling on warm clothes and sipping on a thermos of tea. Enjoying the partial sunset in the distance. Eventually back to the house. Luna said she was hungry, I'd not eaten either. So we agreed to go into town together. Luna took a little while to get ready. Again I didn't know if this was a hint. Was she trying to look her best for me? Or just women wanting to look good any time they're out in public? She asked if I was gonna dry my hair. *"Doesn't it just do that naturally? Like, over time? But that reminds me, I should change into dry underwear"*. Me with dry underwear, Luna with her hair back down and finally ready* booked a taxi. She brought us to a currently Oktoberfest themed pub, with a fancy beer selection and good pub grub. The choice was perfect. I learnt Luna was vegan, and Luna learnt I was vegetarian. I probably downplayed how poor of a vegetarian I was. So the food worked for both, washed down with some quality German beers.

*It was only like 20 minutes getting ready. But that seems like an eternity to a guy who spends approximately zero

345

minutes on his appearance each day. Because even if he does his hair, he's just gonna put a cycle helmet on 2 minutes later to ruin it.

A wonderful evening. The food was probably good? But it was one of those evenings where I was so engrossed, engrossed in conversation and Luna, I didn't even notice what was going in my mouth. There were fleeting moments of intimacy, like when we got onto music and playing piano. She put her hand in mine to show how tiny her fingers were, very difficult for spanning an octave. But then somehow 90 seconds later we were talking about food poisoning and watery diarrhoea. Definitely missed a moment there. Although Luna actually seemed really into the diarrhoea talk, driving the diarrhoea topic forward. Which just made me like her all the more. After a few pints we grab a taxi and head back.

Back at the house we kept chatting. Went through the kitchen and out the backdoor, watched the moon and the stars. Conversation slow and gentle. Wide pauses. Not uncomfortable, both just tired. My brain chugging slowly in the background: Should I "make a move", and if so, how does one "make a move"? I haven't "made a move" for so long. Can you just get away with loudly proclaiming: "Hey! We should totally bone!". Is she in the same boat?

It felt like Luna was "into me" into me. But when it comes to attraction, my people reading skills are about as accurate as trying to pee into the toilet on the last train home, several pints deep. I'm not too worried about rejection embarrassment. For me, it's more embarrassing to not be brave enough to find out. But I'm acutely aware of how awkward it must be for women, who show an inch of friendliness, for it to be repeatedly mistaken for "*I want to sit on your face*". I'd never experienced a holiday host like this. And I didn't want to be responsible for abusing her friendliness. Turning her into a cold, transactional host; like the majority of stays (*maybe I'm being harsh and the majority of hosts are friendly...maybe I'm usually the unfriendly guest. Then in this instance I just really clicked with Luna and came out of my shell?).

Plus it had been such a magical stay, with such a great connection between us. A botched initiation could sour the whole experience. Even if the initiation was reciprocated...it had been a very long dry spell for me. Go back to covid. Go further. Proper Atacama Desert dryness levels. If a footballer had been injured on the sidelines for how long my penis had been out of action, they'd have gone for the humane solution:

- Taking him out back.
- Putting him out of his misery with the shotgun.

Rather than being the cherry on the top; some piss-poor penetration could have been the cold, lumpy, school-dinner custard; ruining an otherwise perfect encounter.

Eventually we ended up on the landing together, next to our respective bedrooms. Silence. Tension of a moment passing by. Like two shits in the night. It reminded me of the time In Newcastle after a Los Campesinos gig waiting for the last bus home. Along it came. Didn't put my hand out; watched it sail off. Into the distance. Into the night. Ended up waiting for the first train home in 24 hour McDonalds. Good lord. 3am Macca's in Newcastle on a friday night has scarred me for life.

Moment slipping past, it was eventually: "*Alright, goodnight then*". "*Goodnight*" and off to our own beds. I sent her a whatsapp message, linking to the "*Mr Lizard*" Jam sketch, explaining the name "Mr Lizard" for Mr Lizard. I couldn't sleep very well, wondering what could have been. Ended up finishing the thankyou note now in the dark, early morning hours. It ended up at about 5 pages. Dove into details of how I'd never met a holiday host like her. Wrote about how she should just also write stuff if she enjoyed it. Might have compared her uniqueness and weirdness to the Aran Islands, this felt a bit cringey. So I tried to divert the cringe by doing a poem for her. It was the "*The Bread Mist Descends*" poem from earlier in the book. Most of it wasn't specifically written for her, but I finished it whilst cycling around Galway. And I thought it might make her laugh so why not xD

So yeah, overall a fairly insane and unhinged note, taped inside the forest card. Left with the other gifts on the bed.

Incredible Ireland: Day 6. Can Bluetac Fix, Bicycle Antics?

With Luna being a late-ish riser, I'd promised not to leave too early in the morning. I used to be plagued by nosebleeds when I was a kid, but they magically stopped at some point. None-the-wiser as to cause, or why they stopped. Suddenly whilst stuffing my bags I felt that familiar runny-nose sensation, but slightly too runny. Doing the dab and seeing "Oh, it's a nosebleed". I'm not a very religious or spiritual person, but I do track the coincidences that occur in life. I hadn't had a nosebleed for maybe 2 years? Why now? I know this isn't logical or rational, but sometimes it feels like the universe is trying to hint you towards the correct path. Especially when the odds of those co-incidences seem so rare. I haven't had a nosebleed since that day either. Particularly peculiar, the one time my nose flows is right when I'm busy packing up. Planning to leave a wonderful house, in a wonderful part of the world, with a wonderful woman*.

*Note: on editing for the 2nd draft I realised I'd had another nosebleed in Antwerp. So it's definitely slightly less of a strange coincidence and symbol. But still, those have genuinely been my only two nosebleeds in the past year.

And it wasn't just this sign. There were more:

- The biblical winds that had pushed me towards Galway.
- The unusual basking sunshine for my whole stay in Galway, incredibly untypical for Ireland in October.
- Said sunshine turning to a dour drizzle as soon as I rode out of Galway county
- As I stopped for lunch whilst riding away from Galway; dropping my super-fancy, £300+ cycling computer. The screen cracking into a million shards.
- The bike literally seizing and falling apart...we'll get to that bit later.

The universe wanted me to bin the plan. Fuck Limerick, fuck Wicklow mountains. Stay in Galway. But I'd paid nearly 100 euros for the Limerick hotel, and changing plans is hard. So I defied the universe. A lovely cup of train her amazing kitchen: filled with houseplants, jars of interest, little Kodama* from Princess Mononoke and a hundred other curiosities. So many little details. But I'd already put myself behind schedule getting to Limerick, and eventually it was a long, tight hug goodbye and back out on the road.

*Cute little white and black forest creatures

I stopped off at the bakery I'd been to the previous day. They did 2 euro bags of day-old leftover pastries, I grabbed 2 of them, should have got more, especially as I'd run out of other cycling snacks, but cest la vie. Coffeed myself and off I went. Just outside Galway, a small town called Oranmore, the bike was already making an alarming knocking sound. It was the same sound I'd been concerned about before the trip, which had stayed dormant in the background until now. But now it had definitely increased in volume, alarming. Each time you pushed the pedals round it would knock, clearly bottom-bracket related. This is bad because bottom brackets are not something you carry tools to fix if it explodes.

But I was already in no-mans-land between Galway and Limerick. Keep going forward. I just crossed my fingers and hoped it would hold together until Limerick. The Burren was stunning. More vast expanses of green and grey. The violent Atlantic to my right. No trees. Just stone and grass. I followed the coastline all the way to the cliffs of Moher*. More hills than I'd faced in Ireland so far, but it was worth it for the scenery, and I was smashing my stale pastries. Progress was fairly slow. I wasn't taking many pictures, but even me, an avid "live in the moment. Not through a camera" just could not resist. I had to remember this place. Even when I wasn't snapping pics I would slow to a crawl just to savour the view. Aran Islands in the far. Desolate black-rock beaches in the near.

*Which did mean I actually missed some of the most "Burren" parts of the Burren further inland.

Approaching Doolin I got the bike over 40mph for the first time I think. Woohoo! Crazy to think that I was scared going above 25mph on the way to Berlin. I was pretty gassed from the hills, running low-ish on food. Needed to stop for a proper lunch. The first pub in Doolin I could hear American country blaring out of. Can't fucking stand country. Might even be worse than jazz-jazz. I love jazz-styles fused into other genres...but pure jazz....does it make my body move and dance? No. Does it fill my soul with emotions and feeling? No. So then why am I listening to it? The only thing it makes me feel is: "Yep, these folks sure can play their instruments well". Jazz is musical masturbation. Eff Jazz.....

(**editor note**: When proof-reading I noticed I already ranted about Jazz in Dublin. However my disdain for jazz is strong enough that it may warrant repeating)

....err got a bit carried away there. Also the same criticisms can apply to some math-rock/progressive-metal. Point was: the first pub was a no-go. Trundled to the next pub. Complete opposite vibe. Dimmed, low lights. Even lower music. It was so quiet, that the staff felt obliged to converse in whispers to match the volume. Their hushed giggles giving the place an eery vibe. Like they were secretly laughing at you. Maybe they were? But they seemed nice and friendly, and I had a nice Salmon salad (once again failing at vegetarianism) with a 0% Guinness and coffee. But definitely a very odd vibe.

This is really the turning point of the trip. The downhill bit. Well in cycling downhill is good. But here I meant getting badderer. Less good. Outside a costly fumble led to the smash and demise of my cycle computer. Well, technically you can still "see" the map on it, through the jagged cracks;

barely. The Cliffs of Moher....they're alright. But....they're just cliffs. I don't know why there were so many tourists. There's similar cliffs on Inish Mor, less tall, but unadulterated, without fences or warning signs.

After the cliffs I was cutting inland towards Limerick. The scenery was still "alright", but it had peaked. And cutting inland I was now facing a meaty headwind. This isn't just wind. This is West Coast of Ireland wind. There's very little protection around. No hedgerows to dampen the onslaught. The bike clunked even clunkyer. The drizzle commenced. I ended up on a really shitty main-ish road heading Eastwards. Packed with cars, all trying to do 70kmh. I really wasn't feeling this road, so dove into a quieter side-road and navigated by feel for a bit. Followed the smaller roads towards Ennis, a town between Galway and Limerick. There was no major time-rush, I hadn't spent long at Moher or the lunch stop. So it wasn't worth it stressing on the busy roads. Learnt my lesson from Anglesey.

The bike was really struggling now. It would sporadically grate on top of the clunking. The grating was like flicking the resistance way up on a spin bike. Mood was dropping as the tiredness increased, battling the wind. Moher the massive anti-climax. I was starting to feel foolish for leaving Galway, leaving Luna without truly probing how deep the feelings were. My mind was flicking through what I could have done differently. Drunk less? I think that with my (self-diagnosed) ADD brain, I'm actually hornier when sober. The dopamine released from alcohol means that once I'm drunk, I just want to keep chasing that dopamine hit. Drinking, partying and chilling the night away. The brain can't conceive of something "more fun" than what it's doing right now. In a society where sexuality is still slightly embarrassing, usually only being surfaced under the loosening effect of alcohol…then never being horny whilst under the influence, is pretty flipping inconvenient. I have a dream…I wish we lived in a world where sober people could just walk up to each other and ask if they can rub their genitals together. And that could happen without anyone cringing or feeling uncomfortable, but alas that's not our world.

When Luna was outside, gazing up at the stars, I could have gone over and seen if she was cold, maybe hugged her. Rather than me sitting in the kitchen doorway like a lemon: "*Are you cold? Yes? That's probably because you're standing outside in the middle of the night. Whereas I am warm and toasty, because I am standing inside the nice warm kitchen.*" :/ I know she loved to dance, so asking her for a dance, either when still in Galway, or back at the house. That could have initiated moments. I was frustrated at only thinking of these things in hindsight.

I'm sure the night before Luna had said "*y'know you could stay if you wanted*" in a way that seemed more than just polite and friendly. I was already thinking about alternative plans. Maybe I could train back from Limerick to Galway. I'd read a whatsapp message from her at lunch which increased how much of an Ejid I felt. Yet still inconclusive as to the way she felt about me. Note: inconclusive to an absolute social lemon like me. Incredibly conclusive to anybody else xD. At least this was something to occupy my mind whilst battling the elements and the bike. Even if it was tinged with a bit of self-loathing.

Eventually around maybe 5pm, I went to pull away from a junction. The bike just went nowhere. The chain had come off. I went to put it back on. As I did, the bottom bracket wobbled an alarming amount. Centimetres of movement side-to-side. I tried putting the chain back on. It fell straight off after two pedalstrokes. On…Off. On…Off. The bottom-bracket was way too loose. It would keep moving sideways enough to knock the chain off. Literally unrideable. If this had happened in the middle of the Burren, it could have been hours walk to civilization. Fortunately I was on the outskirts of Ennis, a mid-sized town.

All the bike shops in Ennis were closed by this time. The only option: try and fix the bottom-bracket myself. There's not really any sensible way to hackily "hold it in place" a bottom-bracket, because the whole idea is it needs to rotate with the pedals.

My smart idea: Blutack. I would stuff the gaps in the bottom-bracket with blu-tack. This would allow it to still rotate, but might hold it enough to stop it from slipping sideways. What a story to brag about to mates: "*Yeah, bike completely fucked itself didn't it....but no probs...I wasn't worried at all. Just bodged it with some blutack didn't I?*". If this worked, I would be a mechanical genius.

The blutack didn't work at all. Of course it was never going to fucking work. And then you know what the worst part about trying to fix your bike with blutack is? Now you've got to sheepishly explain to the bike mechanic in Limerick why the fudge your bike is filled with blutack.

Spolier alert there, I did get to Limerick. Whilst there was no bikeshop in Ennis, there was a convenient train station. So after a 40 minute walk from the outskirts to station, I was Limerick bound, albeit with a broken bike. Glad that I went for a central Limerick hotel. This had been anticipating a wild night out on the town. But came in handy when I needed to walk San there. Was a perfectly fine and boring hotel. What the flip did I eat that night? Can't remember, so it can't have been anything special. Had a small walk around Limerick, grim. Didn't feel like partying, still melacholic after leaving Galway...

Incredible Ireland: Day 7. No Question. San is my Brethren.

...and had to be up early to try and get bike sorted. Walked to the closest bike shop for its 9am opening. The guy had a poke around. Keen to help, but the bottom-bracket type is an archaic style that he didn't have the parts for. He recommended a different shop, 15 minutes trot up the high street. He warned that it was unlikely the other shop could do a "today" last-minute fix, but if they sold me the bearings, then he could finish the job. I motioned to wheel out my bike to bring it to the other shop, but the owner nicely offered for me to leave it there, whilst I went to see if they had the parts.

In hindsight this was him being nice, but not very helpful. As upon reaching shop#2 they said: "*we need to open up the bottom-bracket to see what type of bearings it uses*"...sigh.

Walk back down the high street. Grab the bike. Walk back up the high-street. Sigh.

Being mindful of shop#1 guy mentioning it would be unlikely for shop#2 to sort it today...I employed some cheeky psychological manipulation. I phrased it to shop#2 as:

> "*shop#1 said you probably wouldn't be able to sort it today, but I thought I might as well check*".

So taking it as a direct challenge to their honor, they took the bike in, saying they'd do their best and give me a call.

They did seem like a very busy repair place, small building crammed with bikes of all varieties. had to take the panniers off to walk it through the shop. So I set my expectations low. If the bike got fixed today, that'd be great. But if it doesn't, I can still get the train to Dublin, maybe someone can fix it there. Maybe I can drag it home? Abandoning it had been the plan in Berlin, but I'd been a bit more prepared for that plan. Here I didn't have a good way to hand-carry all the panniers and nick-nacks I'd accumulated (e.g. the flipping massive Lizard). So maybe dragging it was easier than abandoning it? Either way, San had got me through the most important and most epic parts of the trip. He'd put in a good shift. He deserved the love of a good mechanic, not being abandoned in the street to rot and rust.

I sauntered around Limerick, bouncing from cafe to cafe. Sampling a vegetarian lunch place, a fancy bakery pasty, nutella crepe in the milk market, cup of soup. Limerick is not a "bad" town. But it's like when you read an amazing book, or watch an amazing TV series. The one after it just pales in comparison. So going toe-to-toe with Galway, Limerick was always going to come out feeling dour. The rain didn't help. But in general, it lacked the students and tourists that Galway had. Didn't have that same vibe of optimism and positivity in the air.

I read a bit from Intermezzo, but couldn't really get stuck into it whilst waiting for the bike-shop phone-call. If the situations fucked I can handle that. I can make a plan. Being in limbo is uncomfortable, even if I claimed I was relaxed earlier. I wasn't tense, just restless. Around 3:30pm I was getting very bored. I walked to the bike shop to enquire about the bike. I was getting the 2am ferry from Dublin tonight. Did not want to risk my bike getting locked up in the shop. Fortunately when I turned up they had just finished it. Yea boiiiiiii!

With my bacon saved, and with plenty of thanks dispensed, I wheeled it out of the shop. Re-attached all the bags. In my civvie wear, adidas tracksuit and normal shirt. Switched to cycling top, but didn't feel like de-trousering in the middle of Limerick. So off I rolled. San felt so smooth and fluid now. It was fun riding with confidence. No longer picturing him breaking at the worst possible moment, sending us both tumbling down the road.

I only needed to get to Dublin port for 1am. It was around 4pm in Limerick, plenty of time for adventures!

The original plan had been:
- cycle from Limerick to Hospital.
- Take a joke picture with the town sign
- cycle to Limerick Junction
- train to Kildare

- ride from Kildare to the Southern part of Wicklow mountains
- cycle through the Wicklow mountains to Dublin
- ferry home

Maybe I could squeeze this plan into the 9 hours. But we'd be cutting it so tight, and from my experiences with hills yesterday...the Wicklow mountains sounded scary on a time budget. Starting it this late, I'd end up doing all the mountains in total darkness, on a bike with bodgy brakes. Hmmm.

Discretion was the better part of valour. Aka For once I wasn't a total lunatic. We'd ditch the Wicklow mountains part. But I was so happy to have San back to fully functioning (ignore the aforementioned brakes), that I set out to Hospital. It was cross-headwinds again, so tough going. But as I'd eaten a lot through boredom in Limerick, my legs could cope. It was mainly just my arse struggling being in normal trousers. Hospital was only about 25 miles away, so it didn't feel far enough to justify working out where I could change into cycling shorts. Just hopped up out the saddle as often as possible.

Through the Irish countryside we rode, making good time. Drizzle paused. I feel like this was when I had decided that Lucy was not a cool enough name. I had Princess Mononoke on my mind; we'd talked about the film after I noticed the Kodama at Luna's place. She reminded me of the princess, a bit wild. I would not be surprised if one day, she just upped and left for the forest. To live with the forest creatures as one of them. The male main character in Princess Mononoke is Ashitaka. Ashitaka is fueled by burning determination, yet simultaneously a peace-loving individual. Reminds me somewhat of myself. **SPOILERS IN NEXT PARAGRAPH:**

A demon curses him. It manifests on his arm, looking like a massive burn, but making the arm super-strong. I have super strong legs, and what looks like a massive burn on my foot...because it is a massive burn. With me as Ashitaka and Luna as Mononoke, it seemed fitting to re-name the bike to San. The name of Ashitaka's steed. A trustworthy and dependable deer. San would be the perfect name for this bike. So San it has been and San it shall be until it corrodes away, probably after I too am corroded and gone.

Finally reaching the outskirts of Hospital I got a bit distracted, probably thinking about my time in Galway again, and questioning my decisions....."Hey was that a town sign?". I stopped. It would be too funny to blow straight past the sign that was the whole purpose of this mini adventure. So I carefully crossed to the other side of the road and trundled back. Yep, it was, that was close. Hospital is a tiny village with 1 post-office, 1 local shop, 1 church and 1 cow. That's it. The name comes from the Knights Hospitaller who built a church there. But the sign makes for a funny practical joke. Errr...funny might be stretching it. But it amuses me, so...?

I plopped Mr Lizard on my head and took some selfies with the sign. The nearby town cow watched me very intensely throughout the photoshoot. Riding through Ireland made me appreciate how curious cows really are. They do seem like big, friendly dogs in a way (**note**: many people actually die from cow-related deaths in the UK each year, so don't implicitly trust me and do watch out. Don't let a cow into your house. Know your rights.)

After snapping the pics I send my mum the pics with a message: "*I'm in hospital!*".

She did not get the joke. At all.

   "*What have you done now?.....*"

 Seemed more annoyed than concerned if anything….

"*No it's a joke. I'm fine. The sign? The village I'm in? Nevermind.*".

So the joke had fallen flat. Definitely worth the detour…

Joke bombing, it was a short 7 mile stint from Hospital to Limerick Junction. Limerick Junction just seems to exist purely as a train station for routing trains. I guess the clue is in the name. Then we were on board the train, Dublin bound. It felt like the trip had come to an end...but there was one final hurrah to be had.

The full range of Wicklow mountains were off the cards. But I was looking at the map on the train, because maps are fun. The mountains actually start very close to the Southern outskirts of Dublin. I'd witnessed them myself as the ferry had pulled in, slightly alarming me at the potential task ahead. With so much time before the ferry, I could go up the closest mountain (mountain or big hill I'm not sure. Felt like a mountain to me ☐), Ticknock. Could look down upon the mass of Dublin lights from the peaceful woods, then just come back the way I came.

We should end the trip in style. What better way than taking a ridiculously overloaded, already heavy bike, with a flipping 2kg lizard, up a casual 1500ft hill? So through the dark Dublin streets we dashed, over most of the city and out into the suburbs. On the outskirts of the city the gradient gradually picks up, nothing too severe. We get to a bridge over a motorway, already an impressive view of lower Dublin and the sea. Brief enjoyment then a sudden right-hand turning. Small, dark, ominous lane. The gradient kicked immediately. Over 10%. San is already in lowest gear. I was having to stand, grinding the pedals at 40rpm.

Doing our hill dance, throwing San from side-to-side. Sweating and panting heavily. Ascending into the darkness. At some point the gradient went up to over 16%, maybe 20. We were swerving all over the road to give some relief. At one point I just had to jump off and walk. Sort of a defeat, but I was still so far from the top. It was either hop off and walk by choice, or topple over as my legs collapse. With a mix of cycling and walking I reckoned we could make it. Back on the bike we reached the turning where it becomes Ticknock park. I noticed a sign saying: "*Barrier closes at 10pm. Anybody stuck inside will be fined for being released*". A guilty wave of relief flooded me. We're not going to get up and down in time, it's already 9:40. We would have made it, but we weren't allowed. Then I realised we were a bike. Not a car. I could just push San round the barrier. Tried to pretend I hadn't been secretly relieved that we weren't obligated to strive all the way to the top.

Excuse gone, we followed the path into the woods on the hillside. The clouds were low this evening. The summit had one of those towers with red flashing lights, presumably to stop airplanes crashing into it. I was listening to the Princess Mononoke soundtrack whilst we climbed. A great soundtrack, but I'd forgotten how foreboding and menacing many of the tracks are. A super eerie experience.

Completely alone. No Humans. Weaving about, just gradually, yard by yard, inching (yarding?) towards this blinking red light in the foggy distance. Like an Eye of Sauron, or some other malevolent spirit. Blink...blink...blink. Sounds of the forest and its inhabitants. If I'd met some crazy person in the woods I would have completely freaked out and bolted it straight back down. Although maybe I'm the crazy person in the woods?

The climb took almost an hour in total. Tarmac giving way to a gravel path near the crest. I could now see the tower producing the blinking. A low thrum of electricity from a generator next to it, the only sound apart from the howling wind. The earthy scent of evergreen trees. At the top I manoeuvre myself off San, gently lay him down. If it wasn't so cold I would have had a little lie down. Instead I stand and sway. Looking back down, at the expanse of lights that is Dublin. Hundreds, thousands, hundreds of thousands. I could pick out the port, a big stadium, then a sea of pinpricks. People tucked up safe and sound at home. Bars packed with revellers. Cars zipping people from place to place. A fitting finale for an epic trip. An epic year! An epic bike!

I hung around soaking in the sights, patting myself on the back for persevering to the top. Patting San on the saddle for holding it together. Eventually the cold wind started to bite. Then it was back down, ferry-bound. My heart rate had slowed and calmed at the top. But it spiked right back up again on the descent. This was pretty flipping sketchy. I hadn't really thought about the down part. At some point the rear brake started functioning at about 10%, having to squeeze with all your might to get a drop of power from it. Gravity has a pretty large effect on such a bulky bike. A terrifying trip down. Good job I sucked in the sights at the top, as my eyes were glued to the road surface, scanning for potholes. With the back brake failing, I was having to use my shoe. Dragging it along the tarmac. The sole was worn down to the bone. At one point I hit a bump and my braking foot jumped up, whacked the chain-guard. Cut my leg and bent the guard. Nothing too serious, but a definite warning. Being even more steady we made it down in one piece. Heart-rate and adrenaline through the roof. Time to calm down, then a windy route to the ferry. Making sure to stop and load up on snacks for the long way home.

And that's basically it. Slept surprisingly well on the ferry back to Holyhead. Better than hostels or night-trains. Had a 5am ride to Bangor. Rewarded with some more amazing photos of Snowdonia in the distance at sunrise. It did turn into a bit of a time-trial after I realised there was a weird 90 minute gap between trains. And my heart yearned for home after all we'd been through. Rail replacement buses made the journey back even longer and convoluted. But I arrived home safe. Riding San from the station up the big University hill. Turning round to look at Canterbury cathedral down below. The book kind of ends with a whimper. But that's how most cycling trips are. The fun bit has already happened, and then you're just training/flying/whatevering your way home. Relaxed, reflecting on where you've been, what you've accomplished. Trying to stop yourself from plotting the next adventure, just live in the moment for a bit.

Epilogue and Fanks:

Luna and I kept in touch, messaging back and forth. She had a photoshoot in London the next month. She asked if she could stay at mine in Canterbury for a few days. ☐ As if I could say no. Cleared all my plans. Nuked my calendar into oblivion. Let's flipping go!

I don't tend to like books and films with happy endings. Real life doesn't usually have perfect endings. But this year has been a very unreal year for me; closer to fiction than fact, so it feels pretty good this tale does have a happy ending. That reminds me, I need to change my bedsheets (**note to editor**: Surely I can't end on that sentence? ☺ [**editor note**: Guess you can? 😵])

(**editor note**: And even after the Canterbury visit. I'm finishing this off from Shannon airport on 12th December. Yes I crumbled and am flying home. I got well and truly abandoned by Irish Ferries. Cancelling everything with less than a day's notice. Alas I didn't quite manage my flying-free year. There's something distinctly British about coming so close to a goal, only to fall at the final hurdle. We can always pick ourselves up and try again next year. Maybe more, subtle hints from the Universe. The same night I was meant to be starting my epic journey home, Luna's airbnb guest also mysteriously vanished. We didn't murder him. Weird that my ferry being cancelled meant I had to…got to…stay another night in Galway with Luna, and the guest vanishing gave us the house to ourselves. Again I stress: we did not murder him.)

Wow, I can't believe you made it all the way through. What an adventure we've been on. Thanks for toughing it out during the more unhinged sections. Unless you skipped to the end of course. You book-skipping cunt. Nah, you still have a place in my heart.

If you want to be notified of any paperback version, it would help to sign up to my mailing list: thepianodentist+book@protonmail.com. Just ping me an email saying "sign me up boss!" or literally anything sensible.

(**Internet tip**: The `+<anything>@` part of an email address is ignored. So whenever signing up for stuff you can put my.name+shitty_mailing_list@internet.com, and if they give your email to spammers, you can tell who the culprit is.)

Plus any word of mouth, spreading this book, like a virus, to other cyclist friends. Or people who just like adventures in general…yeah, I would be grateful if you'd use your mouth for me. Thanks 👍

Special thanks to Luna for making the Irish trip the trip of a lifetime. Also to Gary. Both wonderful people, and people who inspire me to be a better person in one way or another. Thanks to the Generic Finance Company gang for positive feedback on my writings that made me think it might be worthwhile rambling over 60,000 words down onto paper about my own life oh jeez why does this sentence have no commas or fullstops oh wait here's one. Special thanks to the those involved in London-Paris. Thanks Christian and Dave for a delightful Dutch trip.

Thanks the amazing campsite in Strampoy Netherlands, the amazing bikeshops in Strampoy, Limerick and Faversham for saving my beercans at such short notice. And not featured in this, but Canterbury Evans cycles employees have also done great last minute jobs to save my racing weekends, and in general also go above and beyond. Thanks to my family for "support", I don't think they're too happy with the crazy cycles. But still. Thanks to all the people at the local cycling clubs, CBC and VC Deal. Too many to individually name. Thanks BigBoy69. Thanks to Starcraft Max. Thanks to everyone who helps with East Kent Cyclocross. Thanks to my spin instructors/punishers: Dave and Maxine. And the Canterbury Wattbike crew (Christian and Ben). Thanks to all the wonderful hotels and campsites that put me up, thanks to literally everyone I met and interacted with :)))))))

ThePianoDentist out

note to editor: Put a cool picture here.

Appendix: How to ride your bike really far

- **Build up to it**
  - Adding 10 miles every weekend you can get really far
  - But then for me, it felt like once you can do ~120miles, adding miles and jumping to 150 or 200 actually gets easier. Assuming you are fueling effectively.
    - You'll learn that your body might "give up". But if you just keep going forward, even slowly, if you're well trained enough you'll get a second wind.
- **Be careful with your undercarriage.**
  - Tired legs are not dangerous, and can always be fueld with sugar
  - Infected sores can lead to hospital or worse
  - Give your arse a good feel after every days ride
    - Or ask a friend
  - Use chamois cream if it helps you, multiple times in the ride if needed

- Wash cycling shorts, even if just in showers with soapy water
  - Dry by wrapping in towel and stomping
- Take strong anti-acne face cream and apply to bum at night
- Take athletes feet cream for groin if needed
- Blister plasters if they help.
- Move your arse around on the bike
  - Try to get out of saddle when possible
    - hard with bikepacking bags
  - occasionally push your body long. Makes you aero and takes pressure off your bum
- **Food**
  - Little but VERY often
    - Avoid major meals
  - Start eating early into the ride
  - No set rules, but eating multiple times an hour
  - Easy to digest stuff
    - Pasties are an enemy of mine
    - Fruit and nuts are good
    - Fruit and nut bars as well
    - Looking for high sugar, low fat.
  - Swill your mouth with water after each sugary snack
    - Unless you want a spanking from your dentist

- Also try to stay to harder foods, and not sticky stuff that gets stuck in your teeth
- Proper sandwich is good during a long day
- Incorporate protein especially later on
  - Citation needed but pretty sure your body starts burning it as fuel.
  - Also useful to start repairing muscles post-cycle
- Try to avoid supermarkets without self-service/fast tills
  - you don't want to be stopped for 20 minutes
  - Petrol stations are actually pretty quick and handy
- Avoid proper sit down meals
  - Make sure you're ordering something fast, or just get store stuff
  - Subway/sandwich shops are quite nice
  - Especially during 2nd half of ride
    - your body will not want to get going again if you let it enter recovery mode
- Avoid the "if I don't eat I could lose so much weight trap"
  - You're just going to ruin your big ride/achievement

- Best weight loss results I've seen are from people consistently getting up at 6am and doing daily morning rides. Not one-off big rides.
  - I lost only 0.5kg during this. Pretty sure I'm already putting it back on.
- For multi-day rides, try and get some carbs right after stopping.
  - There's a glycogen window where the body absorbs carbohydrates either faster or more efficiently post-exercise. It's even more important than getting post-ride protein in apparently.
- **Minimise stops**
  - Slow and steady really wins the long bike race. You have to ride way faster to make up what feels like a short stop.
  - Try and combine piss, suncream, chamois, sorting out bottles
- **Drink**
  - the electrolyte tablets are pretty nice
  - Don't go too mental with the "energy powder" in bottles, or you'll not have enough water in the mix and end up dehydrated.
  - The weight of spare water is always worth it

- Bottles with the cap that keeps dirt off :+1:
  - Wash the bottle in hotel/campsite each night
- Your backup bottle can just be a regular/big bottle of water. Can let you carry more.
- **Caffeine**
  - Very useful. Just watch out for crashes.
  - My strategy nowadays:
    - 1 coffee before setting out. This lets you start off at a good pace and "sets the standard" for the day
    - Cool it on the caffeine until half way mark.
      - If you smash caffeine early you can destroy your legs
      - Start smashing it here to bring you up at the stage when your body would be saying "no more please senor".
    - Wind it down near the end. Don't fuck your sleep by smashing coffees when you're less than an hour from the end
- **Bags**
  - Do as I say not what I do:
    - More Pannier bags and no rucksack.
    - Or if you are going to rucksack, at least keep it light

- Voile straps are the best for strapping extra bags to your bike, but regular "straps" work as well.
- **Clothing**
  - Wear cycling shorts, but more specifically cargo cycling shorts with the handy pockets.
    - Jersey pockets are a nightmare for food, as you inevitably fill them with gloves and tat, and you get paranoid about stuff falling out of them when you go for food.
- **Immune system**
  - You are going to be putting your body under load/stress.
    - Extra stress to your immune system and you're just going to come down with a cold.
  - Carry hand sanitiser. Use it.
  - Dont get shitfaced.
- **Satnav**
  - If your route is >100 miles, split it into 100 mile chunks in-case your cycle satnav struggles and lags with really long routes
- **Powerbank**
  - Take a powerbank, so useful for charging lights, satnav, phone.

- Spare lights anyway in-case your main ones break
- **Suncream**
  - Skin cancer is no joke
- **Gear**
  - Pump
  - Multitool with chain-breaker
  - Quicklinks
  - Tubes
  - Puncture repair kit
  - Spare cleat bolts for shoes
  - Spoke tool
    - If one breaks you can remove and tweak the others to get the wheel rideable.
- **Riding style**
  - Avoid grinding up climbs
  - Controversional, but still fine to throw the power down up small kickers
    - Just be sure to do it at decent cadence, and bail into smallring if you've misjudged it
    - occasionally doing small bursts seems to lead to higher average speeds for me. It's not enough to blow my legs. But it is enough to get my heart and lungs pumping, and I can suddenly do a bit faster on the flat. :shrug:

Safety first

☐ If you're riding massive miles, statistically you'll eventually have a driver pull out on you or do something dumb. The only way to keep doing big rides and never end up in hospitable is to either be incredibly lucky, or ride far more cautiously than the average cyclist

Printed in Great Britain
by Amazon

55506967R00219